D1197500

A Man for All Nations

The Story of
Clyde and Ruth Taylor

Carolyn Curtis

CHRISTIAN PUBLICATIONS, INC.
CAMP HILL, PENNSYLVANIA

Christian Publications, Inc.
3825 Hartzdale Drive, Camp Hill, PA 17011
www.cpi-horizon.com

Faithful, biblical publishing since 1883

ISBN: 0-87509-768-5

98 99 00 01 02   5 4 3 2 1

Cover portrait by Karl Foster

Publisher's Statement

Every effort has been made to present the facts of this story
as accurately as possible and to remain true to the history of the
persecution, growth and development of the evangelical
church in Peru and Colombia. The facts can be substantiated
both in South American and North American literature. There
is no intent to malign or wound any church or denomination,
especially in light of the favorable shift in attitude toward evangelicals in Latin America in the last several decades.

Dedication

This book is
lovingly dedicated to

Ruth Marstaller Taylor,
wife of Clyde,

and

granddaughter,
Lori R. Gillikin

Contents

Preface   ix

Introduction: A Story with No Ending   1

1   Horse Sense   19

2   The Lord Always Had His Eye on Me   26

*3   The Lord Never Sent Me Where
I Wanted to Go   36*

4   The Marstallers of Maine   41

5   Cuban Rum   46

6   So This Is Peru   51

7   The Hole in the Wall   58

8   Homesteading in the Jungle   66

9   Angels on the Roof   78

10   You Never Know Who's Watching   85

11   Christmas in the Big House   92

12   White Men versus the Elements   100

13   The Real Enemy   110

14   Prayer Warriors   116

15 Romancing Ruth 125

16 Armenia, Colombia—
A Fighting Chance 139

17 A Price on My Head 146

18 Father Lopez Ups the Ante 156

19 The Missionary versus
the Monsignor 165

20 The Most Unlikely People 170

21 Miracles at the Bible Institute 181

Epilogue 191

Preface

The body of Clyde Willis Taylor lay peaceful and finally free of the cancer that had claimed his life. His family, who had been saying their goodbyes for months, shuffled about, quietly shifting into the tasks necessary after the death of a loved one. A hospice nurse spoke up with some questions. She had been observing this family in her patient's final hours and knew something was different, something was special, something set them apart from the many others she had served. The family of Clyde Taylor had piqued her interest.

One question led to another. It appeared the nurse was unsaved and hungry for the assurance of salvation with which these people seemed so comfortable. Within minutes of his father-in-law's death, Jack Gillikin was locked into a conversation, sharing the gospel, thumbing through Scriptures and reading aloud pertinent verses. The nurse left the house with one of Clyde Taylor's thirty or so Bibles, a gift from his widow of only hours.

And so it went in the life—and the death—of Clyde Taylor. He served as a link between the Lord and people. Those who knew him were not surprised to learn that, even at his death-bed, the gospel was being shared.

In many ways his death scene was a meta-phor for his life. His very presence was fre-quently a testimony of God's grace. For example, in the 1920s during his mission ser-vice in Peru, Indians clinging to upper branches of trees in the thick jungle—out of sight to Taylor and his fellow missionaries—ob-served how these Christian men behaved when they thought no one was looking. Their strong but gentle composure and their sure but sub-missive spirits convinced these savage people to come down from their hiding places and seek what the missionaries were offering.

Years later, as a preacher in New England, Taylor's converts ranged from a man who be-came a prominent college president to a fellow who drove a cab. Both had heard the gospel from this giant of a man with the booming voice and commanding presence, and—what's more—they had seen it lived.

The final decades of Taylor's life, dedicated to presenting an international voice for evangeli-cals, touched the lives of literally millions. Their perspective might not have been heard had it not been for Clyde Taylor whose career mark on the world was to legitimize the large and influential evangelical wing of Protestantism.

It has been a blessing and a pleasure getting to know Clyde Taylor by researching the volumes of news articles written about his work as director of the National Association of Evangelicals and founder and leader of numerous other worldwide groups, by reading diaries peppered with references to world-changing events plus names of international leaders in both religious and political circles, and by interviewing folks whose demeanor changes from businesslike to incredibly warm after my introductory sentence: "I'm writing a book about Clyde Taylor."

Of course, no volume is ever the work of just one person. I could not have accomplished this memoir without the help of many. At risk of overlooking someone, I provide this list: my astute editor at Christian Publications, Inc., Marilynne Foster, the wise and guiding force behind *The Jaffray Collection of Missionary Portraits;* archivists at the well-stocked library at The Christian and Missionary Alliance headquarters in Colorado Springs, who aided my research during my visit and in the months that followed, particularly Dr. Joseph Wenninger and Jean Fuchs; the numerous loving family members of Clyde W. Taylor, especially Orletta Taylor Gillikin, Clyde Donald Taylor, Darlene Taylor Tate and Carolyn Taylor Thompson, several of whom the readers will meet through their comments and memories peppered throughout his stories (including the amazing residents of "Aunt Hill" in Maine, where I spent a restful fall holiday immersing myself in Marstaller lore and reading chapters of this book to Clyde's elderly but energetic wife and sisters-in-law); Clyde's many co-travelers through life, who enthusiastically provided information about his Washington decades and how his missionary work prepared him for that fantastic journey; and, of course, my patient family and friends (including those who prayed me through this project—you know who you are!).

My heartfelt thanks goes to all who contributed their memories, observations and insights for a book I hope encourages others to follow the Lord Jesus Christ, the real Author of all our lives.

Carolyn Curtis
Annapolis, Maryland

Introduction

A Story with No Ending

His work was a permanent legacy. What Clyde Taylor was accomplishing didn't end when he left Colombia. His efforts multiplied and, even today, they just keep on going. It's a story with no ending.

Betty Knopp
Nyack, New York
Missionary to Colombia

Betty Knopp taught at the Bethel Bible Institute founded by Clyde and Ruth Taylor years before her arrival for a lengthy and distinguished missionary career of her own. She is among numerous people willing to share memories and impressions of a young man who entered that South American mission field under sponsorship of The Christian and Missionary Alliance but whose work later in his life knew no geographic, political or denominational boundaries.

Often called "Mr. Evangelical," Clyde W. Taylor for three decades led the powerful National Association of Evangelicals (NAE) whose worldwide constituency numbered in the millions. His bird's-eye view of missions spawned other influential groups, earning him international notice as one of this century's Ten Most Powerful Protestants, a list compiled by United Press International's former religion editor Louis Cassels.

"Today evangelicals have a highly effective voice," wrote Cassels in 1968. He credited Taylor as a pioneer and "the man chiefly responsible for [evangelicals'] growing influence."

Before Taylor was called to the NAE position in Washington, D.C.—an office he opened, expanded and managed—segments of the press and society had referred to evangelicals disparagingly as "the fundamentalists," assuming the Protestant viewpoint on most issues was adequately represented by denominations affiliated with the (then Federal) National Council of Churches. Taylor effectively used the power base he established near Capitol Hill, where he "raised the evangelical banner for the first time and gave us legitimacy," according to Wade

Coggins, who succeeded Taylor at another organization both men served as leaders, now known as the Evangelical Fellowship of Mission Agencies.

"The evangelical movement was not well known and, frankly, it was in some disarray," explained Coggins. "The 'powers that be' in Washington in those days thought the whole Judeo-Christian community was represented by the Catholics, the Jews and the theologically liberal, so-called mainline Protestants, who made up the National Council of Churches. The rest of us were getting lost in the shuffle until Clyde came along. And, besides calling attention to Bible-believing Christians, he was the one who really understood that evangelical Christians should work together to be effective."

When Taylor established the NAE presence in Washington—a position he accepted after his Alliance missionary days in Peru and Colombia (the time period covered in this book) and after several pastorates—his new job, not unlike his first missionary assignment, was to chart the territory. Because there was no precedent for a Washington-based evangelical ambassador or lobbyist, Taylor established NAE's Office of Public Affairs, now called Office for Governmental Affairs.

Thus, it's not surprising that, in speaking on behalf of NAE around the world, Taylor frequently referred back to his own formative days on the mission field. His South American experiences, as readers will learn, tempered him for the demanding decades in Washington.

For example, during his missionary years Taylor was often under physical attack. A price was on his head, a bounty sponsored by the established Roman Catholic Church which was threatened in those years by Protestant evangelicals encouraging believers to read Scripture and pray directly to God. Taylor survived vicious threats to his life; God's grace and perfect timing several times saved him from attackers armed with arrows, machetes, poison, dynamite and other lethal weapons.

His gift for charting new territories—so useful in Washington—became apparent on the mission field. In the 1920s while still a teenager, Taylor and his missionary colleagues penetrated the dark world at the mouth of the Amazon to tame a territory from which no white man had ever emerged alive. They crossed precarious peaks of the Andes on primitive trains, atop mules and by foot. They forded chest-deep rivers. They sawed trees six feet in diameter to build their stations. They risked death by disease, wild beasts and savage people to win souls for Christ.

Taylor docked in South America as a boy and sailed away as a man. Taylor's son wrote:

> *My father served in a Latin America in which the influences of the Roman Catholic*

Church were dominant, where virtually all its priests were foreign and predominantly Hispanic, where Scripture was banned and any other religious option was viewed with open hostility. Fortunately, as the world shrunk and especially with the more inclusive ecumenical and Christian view of Pope John the Twenty-Third, religious liberty eventually developed in Latin America and the attitudes of its people became more open.

Today, evangelicals are the fastest growing religious groups in Latin America and, in many countries, they represent the largest population of regular churchgoers.

Clyde Donald Taylor
Washington, D.C.
son of Clyde and Ruth Taylor
and former U.S. Ambassador to Paraguay

In later years the senior Taylor often referred to his days as a bachelor in Peru and then with Ruth and their children in Colombia. Speaking worldwide as he traveled to more than 100 countries on behalf of NAE and other evangelical agencies, he loved to tell stories of his years as a missionary and what they taught him.

At the time of Taylor's retirement from NAE, Dr. Nathan Bailey, president of The Christian and Missionary Alliance, wrote to the former missionary: "All of us in The Christian and

Missionary Alliance count it a privilege to join
with a host of other friends in extending greet-
ings to you on the occasion of your retirement.
We are not unmindful of the fact that your
Christian service began in The Christian and
Missionary Alliance. The missionary passion,
vision and outreach of those early days have
not diminished through the long years of your
service to the Lord and His Church."

The man who succeeded Taylor as NAE director, Billy Melvin, called him a " true visionary."

"I can't think of a single evangelical organization that wasn't influenced by Clyde Taylor,"
added Melvin. "I always thought that—at
heart—Clyde was a missionary."

Taylor had a talent for management and
founded or helped to organize many of this
century's most effective evangelical groups.

"Clyde threw his arms around us and coun-
seled us in those beginning days," recalled Jack
Frizen of the Interdenominational Foreign
Missions Association.

"We considered him to be a broadcasting
pioneer," said Ben Armstrong, former executive director of the National Religious Broadcasters, which Taylor served as a founder.

Bill Bright, founder of Campus Crusade for
Christ, called Taylor "a gentle giant."

"He was a spiritual mentor and a great statesman," added Bright. "I'll always be indebted to
Clyde Taylor for the time he spent with me,
the wisdom he passed along."

Described as good-natured and physically imposing at 6 feet 4.5 inches, Taylor followed through with the efforts he began and remained actively involved long past his several "retirements." In the 1960s, '70s and '80s, he co-chaired the World Congress on Evangelism, chaired the Latin American Congress on Evangelism and served on executive committees of the International Congress on World Evangelism and the U.S. Congress on Evangelism. He helped to organize the World Evangelical Fellowship. Often in his career he wore more than one hat at a time.

On the occasion of Taylor's retirement from NAE in 1974, Billy Graham, also named on the list of this century's Ten Most Powerful Protestants, said, "The life of Clyde Taylor is not a volume, it's a whole set of books. He did more to bring evangelicals around the world together than any other person. Dr. Taylor did much to inspire me. I had great admiration and affection for him as a personal friend and world Christian statesman."

Indeed, it was Graham's organist, Paul Mickelson, who was among the first beneficiaries of Taylor's influence in the nation's capital. During World War II Taylor worked with the U.S. State Department and Selective Service to establish criteria exempting some of God's servants from military service.

From his modest office near the seat of power, Taylor's vantage point at NAE served as a catalyst for policy changes and activities paving the way for mission work around the world. As a result, missionaries and employees of evangelical groups such as Graham's no longer arrived in distant lands at great expense to themselves and sponsors only to be greeted by letters from draft boards compelling their return home.

Likewise, Taylor interfaced with government agencies to acquire passports and visas on behalf of missionaries, and he assisted governments in reaching church workers scattered throughout the world's most remote regions. Like a true ambassador, his networking highway ran both directions.

> *I worked at NAE during summer vacations from Wheaton College and soon got the Washington bug. While attending NAE's first Federal Service Seminar in 1957, the notion of public service as a Christian vocation crystallized. Years later when I came to the State Department, I discovered it was common to find Dad's business cards on the various countries' desks.*

Clyde Donald Taylor
Washington, D.C.

The senior Taylor's Washington work was far more than administrative. After World War II he negotiated for consensus and a spirit of cooperation among denominations that were competitive on the mission field, sometimes even dysfunctional. He worked on postwar treaties to ensure religious freedom clauses. He made certain that properties seized during wartime were restored to churches. Floyd Robertson of NAE's Chaplaincy Commission said Taylor's work affected the freedom of Christians everywhere to exercise their faith.

"Clyde was privy to God's secrets concerning His plans for evangelizing the world," added Robertson. "Clyde's viewpoint was appropriately broad."

For example, although Taylor was a representative for Protestants who once led a campaign successfully opposing a U.S. envoy to the Vatican after World War II, he also had an appreciation for the Catholic Church's "interest in every matter of welfare, education, labor and science," according to Arthur H. Matthews, whose book *Standing Up, Standing Together* chronicles the history of NAE. Taylor appealed to fellow evangelicals not to make the same mistake as liberal Protestants who, he said, had largely abdicated the role of applying biblical truths to all areas of life.

"Clyde discovered his spiritual muscle when he tackled the potential appointment by President Truman of an ambassador to the Vatican," said Bob Dugan, who became head of NAE's Washington office in 1978. "That move on his part was the opening salvo of evangelical involvement in governmental affairs."

Taylor also understood the servant role of the West in relation to Christians overseas, one of the few Washington insiders with such perspective. Visitors noted that he would forgo office equipment or travel conveniences in favor of funds to feed starving refugee children or to support cases threatening the religious liberties of Christians everywhere.

Indeed, Taylor's big picture approach to problems—leaving the implementation details of his visionary plans to others—and his tight-fisted fiscal management often are the source of amusing, affectionate stories about him.

"Our office staff was never on the cutting edge of technology," chuckles Wade Coggins, recalling NAE's tight budget as managed by Taylor. "When electric typewriters were the norm, we were still working on manuals. And, in fifteen years of traveling with him, I never saw him buy a newspaper. In airport lobbies he would pick up one abandoned by another traveler."

Billy Melvin adds his own anecdote: "We were at a Howard Johnson's in Florida, and, over breakfast, Clyde looked over his notes from the previous day and tried to reconcile his expenses. He was off by 10 cents and it was driving him crazy. Finally, he had a brainstorm and burst out with, "I know what it is! I bought a newspaper and forgot to write it down." I looked up from my eggs and kidded him, 'No wonder you misplaced that 10 cents, Clyde, because you almost never *buy* a newspaper!' "

His boundless energy was infectious but sometimes tiring for people to whom he delegated the tasks his commitments required. Longtime secretary Avery Kendall, smiling years later at her memories of Taylor, said: "He had no idea how long it took to get anything done. He thought we could do anything and everything—which sometimes made things a little difficult."

Because of his height, people sometimes misread him. He was imposing, but when you really got to know him you learned he was a pussycat. In fact, his heart was as big as a watermelon.

When I sensed that people considered him a little unapproachable, I always encouraged them to talk to him anyway. I would say, "Go on up. People benefit from their time with him, and it would be a shame for you to miss such a rich experience." Besides, part of Clyde's greatness was that he listened to and learned from all people, big and small.

Billy Melvin
Wheaton, Illinois
Former Director, NAE

With his finger on the world's pulse and his heart constantly turned to the Lord, Taylor often foresaw political and social problems on the horizon. He sensed the threat of commu-

nism as a sort of "all-encompassing religion" in
the late 1940s and, by the 1950s, was pointing
out the "tremendous promise for evangelical
work" (according to his travel reports) in a relatively unknown Asian nation: Vietnam. He returned to that war-torn country in the 1970s
representing NAE's world-relief arm, bearing
silkworms and fish, plus American experts in
those industries. His foresight and efforts
helped re-establish both the silk trade and the
use of fish farms to promote economic inde-
pendence.

In short, Taylor fully comprehended the com-
plexities of world missions. His conversations,
speeches and prayers were sprinkled with
names of world leaders and locales, political
viewpoints and populations, the intricacies of
global economics plus innumerable facts and
figures. His grasp of information and its significance were both thorough and personal.

"He knew the work of the Lord required
hands-on effort as well as an understanding of
the big picture," said Jerry Ballard of the World
Relief Corporation which Taylor also helped to
organize.

*The calling of evangelicals to responsibility
for and vocations in local, state and federal
government—from Congress to the foreign
service—was not common in the middle of the
twentieth century. Indeed, perhaps in reaction to the theological liberalism dominant in*

mainline Protestant denominations, evangelicals had lost the gospel's emphasis on human needs and social and political justice.

In this context, Dr. Taylor played a pioneering role in helping to redress this imbalance by calling the evangelical church to a more holistic gospel and encouraging greater social and political engagement. Countless college students' lives, including mine, were profoundly shaped by his message, articulated frequently on college campuses, that Christians needed to become involved in public affairs and that politics was a legitimate vocation in serving the kingdom of Christ.

Mark R. Amstutz
Wheaton, Illinois
Chairman, Department of
Political Science, Wheaton College

Taylor's widow, the former Ruth Marstaller, and his four children—Orletta, Clyde, Darlene and Carolyn—recall a family life with a keen awareness of global events. Dinner conversations were peppered with the alphabet soup of organizational acronyms. Guests were frequently the names in the news.

Despite his imposing figure, Clyde also was known for his humility and tender heart. His children recall finding their father often on his knees, a position he assumed for prayer even when, at the end of his life, his body was racked with painful cancer that had spread to his bones.

During the height of Taylor's career his family shared his time with others. The husband and father who was on a first-name basis with world-renowned movers and shakers was frequently absent.

> *We kids thought nothing of answering the telephone at home and finding Billy Graham or some senior government official on the other end of the line.*

> Orletta Taylor Gillikin
> Arnold, Maryland

Taylor traveled to more than 100 countries in his last four decades.

But the first time he left American soil was when he was headed for Peru as, what his family recalls, the youngest missionary commissioned by The Christian and Missionary Alliance. He was only nineteen. And when he set sail he had no idea how many close brushes with death he would encounter.

For example, readers will enjoy his account of one hair-raising Indian raid on the encampment he shared with his fellow missionaries. It was his first assignment and his mission was to evangelize Peru's witchcraft-worshiping Campa Indians. Even in the midst of such life-threatening circumstances, he recognized the opportunities to evangelize. Yet if he missed such a chance, he was hard on himself. He deeply regretted missing an opportunity to win Colombian youths to Christ by not spending time with them on the baseball field after he had stopped them from literally stoning him to death.

Evangelizing was Taylor's true life work. After their return from the mission field, he and Ruth served a church and held other pastoring assignments, including the chaplaincy at a boys' school. Years after the latter job, he and Ruth caught a taxi in Washington, D.C. At the end of the ride, the driver turned to his passengers and said, "Don't you remember me, Dr. Taylor? I was one of your boys." The cabbie then shared the way his life had gone in the years since his youth when Taylor's sermons so molded his direction. "Then we had a word of prayer right in that cab," recalls Mrs. Taylor. "It was so encouraging to Clyde to know those boys were still living for the Lord."

A prominent man in evangelical Christian circles today, Charles Sherrard MacKenzie, considers himself to be one of Clyde Taylor's converts.

In 1941 I was just entering college as, frankly, a pretty mixed-up teenager. One night I heard some church music spilling out onto the Quincy, Massachusetts street where I was walking, heading, as usual, absolutely nowhere. For some reason I wandered in,

climbed into the balcony and heard this min-
ister named Clyde Taylor preach the gospel
more clearly than I had ever heard it ex-
pressed. I had come from a very liberal Prot-
estant background and so this message
touched me deeply.

During prayer at the end he asked people
who were making a Christian commitment to
raise their hands. Tentatively, I raised mine.
But he must have been peeking, because,
when the benediction was over, I was embar-
rassed and tried to bolt, but guess what? He
beat me to the door!

He pumped my hand and welcomed me to
the family of God. That began a lifelong influ-
ence on me. I had a thousand questions about
such issues as the concept of Satan and the in-
errancy of Scripture. As a young philosophy
major, I wanted to know: Can the Bible really
be trusted? Clyde Taylor answered every ques-
tion with his typical thoroughness and pa-
tience. I stayed in touch with the Taylors
throughout my work on theology degrees at
Princeton and my subsequent career as an
educator. I'll always treasure their friendship.

Charles Sherrard MacKenzie
Maitland, Florida
President Emeritus of Grove City College,
current professor of philosophy
and advisor to the president
of Reformed Theological Seminary

Travel with us back to an earlier part of the twentieth century when Clyde W. Taylor grew up and eventually took his place among the many other distinguished missionaries who risked life and limb to bring the gospel to a fallen world.

1

Horse Sense

Nostrils flared and eyes blazing against the pitch black night, my father's horse reared up in defiant protest as they reached the railroad bridge.

It must have been a scary scene for the animal pulling Dad's buggy. The narrow line of rails stretching across the Arkansas River formed the only boundary between the horse's hooves and the cold waters rushing below the rickety span. Even a horse has sense enough to recognize the danger of stumbling on the wooden ties or the rails which hugged the ragged edges of the bridge.

That old beast had pulled Dad's buggy enough to know that the weight of it would have plunged the whole contraption—buggy, driver, horse and all—into the choppy river. He

neighed loudly and convincingly, front hooves
boxing the cool night air.

But Dad's whip prodded the faithful animal
to take a first tentative step onto the railroad
track. And then another step. And then another. The neigh became a soft whinny as my
father's will prevailed over the pounds of horse-
flesh in front of him. Together they crossed the
Arkansas River and brought back the man
whose prayers would save my life.

My name is Clyde Willis Taylor. From the
time I was born on November 7, 1904, in Fort
Smith, Arkansas, events were taking place that
would impact my whole future. The Lord
seemed to have His hand on me even from the
very beginning.

Applying some hindsight, for example, I see
that the desperate circumstances which
brought my father and his horse-drawn buggy
to a rickety railroad bridge spanning the Arkansas River were more than a precarious trip to
the other side. It was the beginning of a journey for my whole family. And it was the point
in my life when the hand of the Lord first inter-
vened on my behalf.

It seems I was not too strong as an infant,
and, by the time I was only five or six months
old, I had picked up malaria and dysentery.
The water was bad in Fort Smith. In fact, in
those early days, water-related illnesses were
common throughout the Arkansas River valley.

Doctors often had to deliver the hard news to parents that their youngsters might not survive once they caught such debilitating illnesses.

And that's just what the doctor told my parents after I had suffered for months with the chills and fever characteristic of malaria and the continuous diarrhea which accompanied dysentery. By the age of one, my fragile body was still unable to kick the sporozoan parasites in my red blood cells (the cause of malaria) or the infection attacking my intestines with a vengeance.

It looked bad. During one particular house call the doctor sadly told my parents he doubted I would live through the night. But my parents weren't ready to give up on their only child. My father, forty at the time of my birth, and my mother, thirty-one, had been wanting to start a family after much moving about the country in search of stable work. Now they were settled—or so they thought—and little Clyde, sickly baby that I was, was their long-awaited first child.

I wish I could say that my parents were strong Christian believers who knew the ways of the Lord at this point, but I cannot. Fortunately, those days and that understanding were ahead in the life of my family. Yet even then my parents felt the pull to call on God in their time of need. And, with me sick and dying on a bed in our humble Arkansas home, this was just such a circumstance.

They had heard of a black preacher known to pray for sick people who then often got well. Trouble was, this man lived on the other side of the Arkansas River, a bit of a journey in those days. The closest link was the old railroad bridge.

My father hitched up his faithful horse to the family buggy and headed out into the dark night. No street lamps illuminated their way; the stars and the moon provided the only light. And the bridge, of course, was built to accommodate a heavy train rumbling high above the icy waters below, so no secure side railings existed to settle the nerves of a skittish horse. It must have been quite a ride, because, once on the other side of the river, Dad had to find the preacher's home, convince him to return to our house and promise to bring him back. And all this while Mom tended to the object of this flurry of love and activity—namely, me—who lay dying an excruciating death. Would I last till Dad got back?

By 10 p.m. horse and buggy, plus passengers now numbering two, arrived back home to my frantic mother and her rapidly declining one-year-old.

In their anguish and the excitement of the moment, my parents never recorded the name of this dear old preacher who sat them down and talked to them for almost an hour. In that time, he exacted from them almost every promise he could think of and they agreed:

that they would raise me for the glory of God, that they would accept Christ as their Savior, that they would hold family worship in our home. I'm sure they were ready to promise him anything if he would just get down to the praying part of his visit.

Finally, he did. The old man prayed and prayed. Late into the night—the very night our doctor had said I would not survive—the preacher prayed his heart out. He told the Lord my parents would raise me for His glory, would worship His Son Jesus Christ as their Savior and would honor Him with worship in our home. No doubt my parents nodded in agreement. And, after the lengthy heartfelt prayer, my father and his faithful horse delivered the old preacher back to his home on the other side of the Arkansas River, just as he had promised.

The next morning, I'm told, the sleepy toddler awakened and immediately asked for food. It was the first sign of robust health my parents had seen from me in months. And that was the end of my malaria and dysentery.

Shortly after my overnight recovery my folks decided they would move from Fort Smith to Tulsa, Oklahoma, where Dad thought the work opportunities would be better. In the next eighteen months we lived in both Tulsa and San Antonio, Texas, each move precipitated by a search for work. Finally, in 1906 my parents settled in the Territory of Arizona, buying a house next door to their best friends. Our new neighborhood was near the city limits of Phoenix. I came to think of this city as my home.

My father Robert was born in Trenton, New Jersey, of Scotch-Irish parents on January 16, 1864. We never knew much about my Dad's parents or family except that he was the oldest son and ran away from home when he was in his late teens to escape his father's alcoholism. The younger children in his family seemed to have been less affected by this problem and wound up with better educations than my Dad who ended up with only three or four years of schooling.

My mother Mabel was born in Le Sueur, Minnesota on June 3, 1873. She was the oldest girl in the family and, as was the custom in those days, the oldest daughter took over much of the housework from the mother. And so my Mom never really had more than about three years of formal education either. The rest of her time was spent in charge of her family's house.

When she was in her late teens her family sold their farm in Minnesota and moved to Golden City, Missouri, a little village northeast of Joplin. Her younger sisters had boyfriends back in Minnesota and so eventually the girls returned to that state and married. My mother, however, took up a career as a pastry chef in hotels and secured a job near Omaha, Nebraska.

While working at the hotel she became close friends with another young woman who was in charge of the maids. It was to be a lifelong friendship. After my mother married my father and Clyde Ennis (as her female friend was called) married her husband, William Keuling, the two couples moved around the country together, often living side by side as they did in Phoenix. When I came along, the source of my own name was this close family friend.

In the meantime, however, the two newlywed couples explored a bit of the developing West. They moved to Golden, Colorado where my father continued his work as a painting contractor and Uncle Bill, as we called him, opened a small cigar factory.

I probably would have been born there had it not been for what was then considered to be an important breakthrough—an advancement in modern technology so significant that my parents pulled up stakes and moved again.

2

The Lord Always Had His Eye on Me

S omeone had invented the cement block maker, a contraption which facilitated the production of a popular construction material, in turn causing a boom in the building industry. Just as computer chips revolutionized industry at the end of the twentieth century, the concept of mass production in the infancy of this century was considered a major labor-saving development for American business. And, just as today, fortunes were made (and sometimes lost) by people with the vision and foresight to recognize such commercial potential.

My father seized the opportunity, leaving his job as a painter and taking a franchise to introduce the cement block maker to another part of the country, a territory spanning western Arkansas and eastern Oklahoma. They moved to Fort Smith and my Dad established a business constructing houses.

After my miraculous recovery from malaria and dysentery, they followed the construction opportunities to Oklahoma and Texas, eventually settling in Arizona, where the two families purchased five acres and decided to go into the strawberry business. The two women—my mother and the friend we referred to as my aunt—managed the farm interests. My father continued in construction, now concentrating more on carpentry as his personal skill, while Uncle Bill went back into the cigar business.

Curiously enough, in spite of all the promises my folks had made to that black preacher back in Arkansas, I have no recollection of going to church or Sunday school as a little tot. And we certainly weren't having family worship services in our home as they had agreed when my life seemed to hang in the balance at the tender age of one. Again, however, the Lord delivered me back to my parents even though they were not living up to their prayerful promises.

The young city of Phoenix was carved out of the desert in a territory which during the opening years of this century had not yet achieved statehood. It was wild and bone dry. Water was provided by way of irrigation ditches bisecting the city. Not a safe place for a boy to play!

One day I tumbled into a ditch and was swept half a block downstream before I was caught in one of the dams. The gushing water trapped me there and no one could hear my screams for help. When my parents began to miss me, a frantic search began. They found me just as I was losing the strength to keep my head above water and pulled me out before I drowned.

Again, it seems in retrospect that the Lord always had His eye on me even though my family was not serving Him at that time.

My health problems continued. At age six, just as I was about to enter first grade, I came down with a bad case of tonsillitis. The doctor didn't want to operate until the inflammation in my throat was reduced. So, for almost a whole year I stayed home having my throat painted or some other treatment until the doctor was able to remove my tonsils.

My health immediately improved and, in the fall of 1911, I was enrolled in a one-room country school near the outskirts of Phoenix where the two families now had a more expansive farm which included orange groves and pastureland. And, although I had been recuperating at home during the previous year, I had been reading, practicing my writing and solving arithmetic problems. So, when I enrolled, I was

promoted immediately to the second grade because I already had mastered those basic skills.

It was soon after my enrollment in school that
a tremendous event took place in the life of our
family. As I have indicated, my folks were not
regular churchgoers. But they became interested
in the highly publicized arrival in Phoenix of a
former priest named Father King, a dynamic lec-
turer with a nationwide following who packed
out auditoriums. His message was controversial.
No church was willing to risk renting their building to him, so Father King rented the Phoenix
Opera House. In fact, everywhere he went he
was accompanied by two big Irish bodyguards
openly armed with .45 revolvers. And people all
over town including my parents wanted to know
why.

At first it was shocking to hear, but Father
King, quite frankly, was denouncing the teach-
ings of the Catholic Church. He was talking
openly about how he had found Jesus Christ as
his Savior and how, contrary to Catholic teach-
ings of those days, he encouraged his followers
to read the Scriptures for themselves and to
pray to God for themselves. These were hereti-
cal notions, and Father King's lectures were fo-
menting plenty of discussion around town.
(Little did I know that, as a South American
missionary only a few years later, I myself
would engender similar controversy!)

My parents were caught up in the excitement and promptly signed up for the Opera

House lectures, the closest meetings to re-
vival they had ever attended. Well, the Lord
got hold of both of them, and when they arrived home they were talking about how they
had gotten "saved" in the meetings of that famous ex-priest. Our life as a family was for-
ever changed.

Their first concern after that was to find a
church where they could learn more about the
gospel. The nearest church to our home, the
First Missionary Church of Phoenix, was
known simply as the Missionary Church. It was
a little brick building only three blocks away.
And so my folks went there and found that
they were preaching the gospel. From then on,
practically every time the church doors were
open, we were there. My father became one of
the trustees of the church and sang in the
choir. My mother taught a Sunday school class
of boys. And we had family Bible study and
worship every evening after supper. I was only
seven at the time. Soon my only sibling, Harold
Grant Taylor, came along.

Eventually, there were a few other moves, including some to California, but whenever we
were living in Phoenix we attended the little
Missionary Church.

I was about fifteen when I talked my folks
into allowing me to apprentice as a carpenter. I
liked to work with my hands, so my Dad got
me a job with one of his contractor friends.

During my second summer on the construction crew a horrible accident occurred. One day, as a team of burly men struggled to carry a huge, load-bearing beam, suddenly one of the men tripped. The next thing I knew the men were plunging toward me at a dizzying speed. The enormous beam came rumbling over my legs, fracturing both knees and causing damage severe enough to keep me out of commission for months.

Although my body was young and should have healed rapidly, the breakage was massive. Doctors did all they could, but it appeared I would be in pain for months and might limp for the rest of my life. In addition to bringing to a sudden end my summer job, the accident cost me participation in two high school activities I loved: athletics and military training.

It was during this frustrating recovery, when doctors seemed unable to ease the pain, that I accepted Christ as my Savior. Although it was a decision I certainly did not regret, it had its consequences as far as my popularity with high school friends was concerned. Many turned their backs on me. It was a painful time both physically and emotionally for a young fellow who had been a star athlete and who was fit enough to work alongside grown men on a construction crew. Still, I was rejoicing in the Lord and became involved in the YMCA, one of the few Christian organizations for young people in those days.

One Sunday three or four months after the accident, our minister was preaching on the book of James. His sermon topic was the relationship of prayer to sin. In the course of his study he read aloud the thirteenth verse of the fifth chapter. And then he skipped to the fifteenth verse before concluding his reading for the day with the sixteenth verse.

I was following along in my Bible and noticed what he had done. *Why?* I wondered. *The fourteenth verse sounds like something I could be very interested in!*

Verse fourteen talked about anointing people with oil and praying for them if they were sick. And I had two very sick legs. For the first time in months I was excited and hopeful.

After the service I talked to my mother.

"Why didn't the pastor talk about the fourteenth verse?" I asked.

Mom startled me with her answer.

"Why don't you go to the minister and ask him yourself?"

I thought about what my mother said: "Go up and ask him for yourself."

"Is any one of you sick? He should call the elders of the church to pray over him and anoint him with oil in the name of the Lord" (James 5:14). The fifteenth verse went on to say that the "prayer offered in faith will make the sick person well."

I knew what Mom was thinking. In the ten years or so since she and my father had come to know the Lord they had given birth to a second son and had watched as their first son (me) also had accepted the Lord. No doubt they were emotionally wrenched when this devastating accident seemed to spell the end of my days as a physically active young man. Yet my mother knew this Bible verse gave me hope for a full recovery. I could participate again in sports. I could participate again in my high school's military training. Both would be important activities for a youth who recently had sacrificed some popularity among his peers by declaring himself to be a Christian.

But what if the church elders refuse my son's request to pray over him and anoint him with oil in the name of the Lord? Will Clyde's faith remain strong? she must have been wondering. Urging me to follow my instincts and speak to the minister about this verse was a gutsy thing for a mother to do! She watched me out of the corner of her eye as I made my decision. As usual, I struggled to stand up on my badly crippled legs. Then I limped up to the minister who was still standing near the communion table as the sanctuary cleared of worshipers.

"Why are you so interested in that verse, Clyde?" he asked me.

"You know I've got this problem with my knees," I answered. "They're definitely 'sick knees,' and, well, I just wondered if the verse really meant what it said."

I held my breath while I waited for his answer. I didn't have to wait very long.

"I believe it means exactly what it says, Clyde. Do you want us to pray for you?"

I had never seen anyone anointed with oil and prayed for in the church before, although, from his answer I gathered that it was something that was practiced when requested.

I gave him an enthusiastic "yes."

Just then, one of his daughters passed near where we were standing. He called her over and instructed her to go to the front of the church where folks were still shaking hands and saying their goodbyes and to gather up some of the deacons (our church didn't have elders). She returned in a few minutes with five men. He sent her off again on another errand: to run next door to the parsonage to get a bit of olive oil from her mother. She disappeared obediently and soon returned with the oil.

The pastor asked the deacons to join me in the front pew where I had settled down to get the weight off my constantly screaming knees. He then explained why I had come. Everyone listened intently as he read aloud the passage from James and gave instructions. He suggested that we all have a time of prayer. We all bowed our heads.

"Clyde, do you have any unconfessed sin in your life?" the pastor asked.

I told him I didn't as far as I knew.

He instructed me to kneel. My knees were

incredibly swollen to about three times their normal size. Plus, they were so inflamed they felt like they were on fire. But I got down on them anyway. The pastor prayed, "Now, Lord, You know all about this. You've heard our prayers. You know what Clyde's trouble is here with his legs. We're going to anoint him with oil. We ask You to heal him immediately."

He took the olive oil, just a simple product from his wife's kitchen cabinet, and dabbed it on my forehead. At that moment I felt a sort of shock go through my body. I rocked back on my heels. It was a miracle! My knees had shrunk back to their normal size and the inflammation was completely gone. And my knees have been normal ever since—with one exception: I have no reflexes in my knees, which always bothers doctors when they give me physical examinations. But it provides a natural opening in the conversation about my medical history to tell them why.

I think of my father as strong and robust, a budding people manager, even as a teenager. I know he supervised about fifty Mexicans who worked on the construction crew. His recovery from the accident must have been remarkable, because he went on to play basketball in college.

Clyde Donald Taylor
Washington, D.C.

3

The Lord Never Sent Me Where I Wanted to Go

The miraculous recovery of my knees was the turning point in my life as far as my commitment to serve the Lord was concerned. Until then I had hoped to become a mining engineer—a growing profession in Arizona where there were numerous mines—because I was comfortable with math and science and because my state had one of the most prominent mining schools in the country. But the Lord had other plans for me. He wanted me to serve Him professionally, probably as a missionary to Africa—or so I thought.

When I finished high school at seventeen, my Sunday school teacher encouraged me to attend the Missionary Training Institute (MTI) in Nyack, New York, an educational center of The Christian and Missionary Alliance. I knew that this missionary denomination with which my Phoenix church had affiliated was committed to worldwide evangelism and discipleship as reflected in its determination to plant churches around the world.

It made sense for me to enroll in this well-respected school if I wanted to learn from the best and to live among students who would be twentieth century leaders of world evangelism. Nyack, as the institute was called, had high standards. It trained and sent into service only those Christians who were sound in their faith, filled with the Spirit of God and energized with a passion for reaching people who did not know Christ as their personal Lord and Savior.

I'm only a teenager, I thought. *Am I up to the task?* After much prayer and discussion with my family, I applied to Nyack and was accepted.

In late summer 1922, I made my first cross-country trip by train to enter MTI in September. As the familiar deserts of the southwest faded, vast wheat fields of the central United States came into view and, finally, the lush greenery of the east filled the horizon. I eagerly pressed my face against the window of the rushing train. *What a blur of sights and feelings!* I thought to myself. *And I haven't yet set foot outside my own country.* I pondered a future to be spent sharing my increasing faith with people of distant lands.

I had no idea such work would be controversial and that one day I would have a literal price on my head. Men would hunt for Clyde Taylor in exchange for bounty money, relentlessly pursuing me with machetes and poison. To stone me would become the obsession of young boys. To kill me would be the direct orders of men who claimed they were serving God.

At Nyack I grew physically as well as spiritually. In my first year I shot up almost six inches. By the time I graduated from the two-year course, I was 6 feet 3 inches. At nineteen I still hadn't reached my full adult height which would be 6 feet 4.5 inches. In fact, my height was deceiving. I was exceptionally young for a Nyack graduate ready to go to the mission field, but I was plenty large in size. The question was whether I was mature enough for missionary service.

The answer seemed to come from an opportunity to teach Spanish at Nyack while I continued with further studies there beyond the missionary training program I had already completed. As a youngster living in the American Southwest I had grown as comfortable with Spanish as with the hot-peppered dishes cooked by our Mexican neighbors. So I accepted the challenge to help my fellow students learn this language spoken in so many countries where the Alliance sent missionaries.

Meanwhile, I was sure my destination was Africa.

In October 1924 a special appeal came for missionaries to go to Peru to work among the Campa Indians. We were told that the Campas were a particularly savage tribe located deep in the heart of thick, uncharted Amazon River jungles from which no *anglo* (person of European descent) was known to have emerged alive. The fact is that the Alliance leaders combed through the candidate list in search of single men to answer this call because they figured women wouldn't dare go into territory so treacherous.

Being determined to go to Africa, I was totally surprised when I was called before the board and asked if I would go to Peru. This was the first of a chain of events which led me to eventually conclude that the Lord never sent me where I wanted to go. Looking back, I can't remember one single exception. And yet today I honestly can say that what resulted from my following the Lord's plans for my life always turned out to be for the best.

The leader of our team to Peru had already been selected. He was Ray Clark, a former missionary to Brazil who was currently living in Jamaica. The search for three single men continued at Nyack.

Of the three men in my graduating class of 1924, one was an engaged fellow. The board assured him that after we were settled in Peru they would see about bringing his wife if the couple would agree to postpone their wedding. His fiancée talked him out of it and so his name was dropped from the list.

The other man was Ben Barton, a fellow student who was quiet, deeply spiritual and very dedicated. He had enormous willpower and self-discipline, two important traits for such a physically and spiritually demanding assignment. Ben was about twenty-eight (nine years older than I) and came from a large family that lived in Aroostook, way up in the potato country of northern Maine. Ben accepted the call.

They had run out of names of single men from my class so they looked to the class of 1925. A standout was thirty-one-year-old Charlie Marstaller, another Maine native. Charlie had been studying Spanish and had applied for work specifically in South America. We agreed that Ray Clark, Ben Barton and myself would go ahead and that Charlie Marstaller would join us in a year.

When I set sail, I never dreamed that Charlie's addition to our missionary team a year later would provide a significant link to my future.

4

The Marstallers of Maine

Charlie Marstaller was older than I, but he was physically fit and could run like the wind. His fleet-footedness came in handy on April 1, 1905, when, as an energetic twelve-year-old, Charlie ran a solid four miles to fetch the family's midwife. His mother, who eventually would bear twelve children, was ready to deliver her tenth. With no telephone on their remote Maine farm, Charlie took off on foot. He delighted in telling the story every year on his sister Ruth's birthday.

Charlie was to become my lifelong friend and future brother-in-law. Of course, as the Lord always does, He was planning for decades and maybe longer the circumstances that would join our two families together by marriage.

The Marstallers were of German ancestry. My future father-in-law came to this country as an orphan of fifteen. It was not uncommon for young people in the late 1800s to be on their own at such a tender age considering the short life expectancies of adults. However, I have no doubt that spending his youth as an orphan had a great impact on the senior Marstaller's character as a grown man—which is when I had the privilege of knowing him. For example, although he worked with his hands, this man was sensitive enough to share openly that he often felt the hand of God giving him guidance and a sense of security as a youngster alone in this world after his parents died. So when he arrived in America with no earthly parents, he nevertheless had a strong relationship with his Heavenly Father. After landing in New York harbor, he made his way to Texas and got a job as a farmhand. Eventually, he found a wife and started a family. Later, they moved to Durham, Maine, where they purchased a farm.

Farming was our way of life. I knew how to weed, that's for sure. As soon as I was old enough, I learned the business end of a hoe. By the time I came along as child number ten there were plenty of family stories about growing up on farms in Texas and later in Maine. One winter morning after the move up north, a child in the family looked out our window and saw the ground covered with mysterious

*white stuff. She cried excitedly, "Mommy,
look! God sent us some cotton!"*

Ruth Marstaller Taylor
Durham, Maine

Farming sometimes could be a cruel way of
life providing a fundamental economic lesson
in the law of supply and demand. One season,
for example, the Marstallers ate rice instead of
their own delicious homegrown potatoes because the market price per bushel was too high
to waste a single spud.

The spiritually strong Marstaller family was
active in The Christian and Missionary Alliance Church and often attended Alliance-
sponsored conferences held at the camp
ground at Old Orchard Beach, Maine. Along
with as many as 5,000 others, they fanned
themselves in the summer heat and listened
for hours to sermons by A.B. Simpson and
Joe Evans. The Marstallers were prominent
Alliance members and were on a first-name
basis with its leaders.

Their son Charlie was the first of five of the
Marstaller offspring to go to Nyack, including
his sister Ruth who would enter my life during
my first furlough from Peru. Her strength was
what I needed for the missionary duties that
were ahead of me in Colombia where living
conditions were not as primitive as in Peru but
where fierce spiritual battles would be fought. I

needed a helpmate. The Lord was preparing Ruth right from birth.

Her mother, who confided in Ruth that she had never learned to read, made sure her husband read the Bible aloud every evening after supper. After their family Scripture lesson, the older children would resume their school studies around a large mahogany dining room table which was expanded to accommodate all the youngsters. On one snowy evening Ruth's father came to her bedroom where, as a six-year-old, she already was tucked in for the night.

> *Gently and lovingly, my father talked to me about the Lord. He asked whether I wanted to invite Christ into my heart. I told him "yes." He led me in a simple prayer appropriate for a child. I remember the light shining on his face from the fireplace in my bedroom. His eyes just seemed to sparkle.*
>
> Ruth Marstaller Taylor
> Durham, Maine

I later marveled at Ruth's stories about growing up with so many siblings—always someone to take care of the younger ones when the parents were busy and enough kids to form a team for most any game. What a contrast to my family with only one younger brother and myself!

Ruth's father liked to tease his children by kissing them after he came in from the frigid Maine winters with ice encrusted on his mustache. His cold, bushy hair against their soft faces elicited childlike squeals and giggles of joy.

Both parents believed in hard work. Ruth's father would work until his own perspiration sloshed in his shoes. Ruth's mother had handled most of the household duties when she was a child—she made a kettle of cornbread for her whole family when she was only six!—and she believed that sharing responsibilities was practical experience in a large family. (When Ruth and I had to build our own mission station years later in Colombia, I was glad she knew how to wield a hammer.)

And, like my family, hers openly called on the Lord in times of danger or sickness. Once, for example, when Ruth had measles and ran a high fever, her father prayed continuously from late morning until 4 o'clock in the afternoon.

Disobedience wasn't tolerated. She remembers a spanking she received when she told a lie. Knowing Ruth, I imagine that's the last one she ever told.

It's comforting to know that, while I was whacking my way through dense Peruvian jungles, learning the realities of manhood and missionary work and all else that the Lord was willing to teach me, He was preparing this charming young lady to one day be my wife.

But that was still several years off. First, I had to get to South America.

5

Cuban Rum

Travel to my first overseas assignment in Peru included a five-month detour to Jamaica where our team convened to learn about tropical agriculture and medicine under the tutelage of our leader Ray Clark.

A missionary with one term in Brazil already under his belt, Ray had married a Brazilian woman who later died in childbirth. Ray returned to his homeland of Jamaica where his father was a judge and his brother and sister, both married and well entrenched in Jamaican society, still lived. This was to become our extended family during our introduction to the tropics.

Just getting to Jamaica was an adventure. Travel information in the 1920s could be unreliable. I was advised to take a ship from the port of New Orleans to Havana, Cuba, where I would catch a second passenger ship to Kingston. In reality, it was not that simple. After traveling the entire length of the Cuban island by train and waiting about five days in Santiago, I discovered that the only passage I could get to Jamaica was aboard a freighter loaded with supplies and one seasick passenger—me.

The time spent in Santiago was not wasted, however. While hanging around my hotel checking on the daily schedules of boats, I ran into a young man I had known back in Phoenix. He now represented the National Cash Register Company and was in Cuba to service the machines. I had plenty of time on my hands, so he took me around with him to make service repairs where necessary.

One customer was the Baccardi® rum factory. As usual, we spent our time in the office area where the machines were located. After he completed his maintenance check, my friend and I were offered a tour of the plant. That afternoon I learned more about how rum is made than I ever cared to know, and at the end of the tour the factory official offered us each a bottle of their very finest. I recognized it to be an act of both marketing and generosity and so I accepted, although I knew I had no particular use for the stuff.

When we left the plant I offered my bottle to my friend, but he declined. So I took it back to the hotel, carefully wrapped it in a paper sack and set it aside. Later, I gingerly laid the wrapped bottle of rum among other items in my trunk, cushioning it with clothes, so that it made the trip safely with me to Jamaica and eventually to Peru, where I promptly forgot about it. I don't know why I took such good care of that bottle, but I did. Funny thing is, years later I put that rum to very good use.

Our Jamaican training included agriculture (we would be growing bananas, cultivating various Peruvian vegetables and generally growing our own food); construction (besides literally cutting our way through the jungle, we would be building our own bamboo and mud shelter, a combination mission and house); and medicine (we would be on our own to diagnose tropical diseases such as typhoid and malaria plus the maladies people have all over the world and, in most cases, left to treat ourselves, including self-administered injections). So our time in Jamaica was essential to our success.

We also needed to learn about witchcraft. Most Jamaicans, even professing Christians, were involved in witchcraft in one way or another. We knew we would encounter demonic forces in Peru where the savage Indian tribe we (hopefully) would be converting worshiped *things* rather than *God*.

What we got in Jamaica was an education in the supernatural. We soon and forcefully learned that Satan was alive and well and operating openly in the lives of people who did not oppose him. For example, we saw rocks the size of oranges being thrown by unseen forces and from unseen places. When we approached the rocks we found they were too hot for a human to handle. They were almost on fire! And they had been hurled through the air as far as 150 yards—too far for a human to toss anything! We also met a girl known to be demon possessed who could predict where and when these rocks would be thrown.

So I began to realize that soon I would be moving into a jungle territory completely under the power of the enemy of my soul and that I was going to have not just a physical tussle with my new surroundings but a spiritual one as well.

But let me jump ahead in my chronology and finish the story about the Cuban rum.

One day after we were well established in our life in the Peruvian jungles, our Indian neighbors brought to us a woman who had been bitten in the head by a banana snake, an extremely poisonous variety with a bite that could be fatal. This woman had been carrying on her shoulders a freshly cut bunch of green bananas large enough to hide the snake. She was in terrific pain and was failing fast. And, unfortunately, we had run out of the serum to fight snake bites.

Suddenly I remembered something I had learned a year or so earlier while we were training in Jamaica: alcohol sometimes offsets the poison of snake bites. It was worth a try.

I searched everywhere for that bottle of Cuban rum and finally found it wrapped up and stored near the bottom of my trunk where I had left it. I opened it, took a whiff and discovered that it still smelled like the bad stuff that it was. The trouble was that we had to literally get this woman drunk to make sure we had put enough alcohol in her system to counteract the bite.

The woman survived. In fact, she became one of our converts. I think that's the only time in my life that I ever had anything to do with alcohol. After that day, I junked the bottle. It had done its duty.

6

So This Is Peru

Last in the fields the Alliance entered in Latin America is Peru. The valiant party of the first three headed for what a missionary leader has termed "the most heroic missionary field of the world" is now in Peru, studying Spanish and planning to move on into the interior. Admirable preparation has been made by the training of this party for the life of the tropical jungle in Jamaica through the generosity of Jamaican members of the Alliance. A deadly epidemic reported to be of yellow fever now rages in the territory they propose to enter. It is not surprising that the powers of darkness are aroused, but they have been conquered, and the challenge comes to those who stay.

Excerpted from *The Alliance Weekly,*
July 25, 1925

We concluded our stay in Jamaica a little early and left in May of 1925 by ship for Panama and then on to Lima, Peru. When we arrived in Lima's port, we were surprised to discover there were no docks, so we anchored out in the bay. Passengers were taken ashore aboard launches, and the luggage was brought about an hour later. Claiming our trunks and other baggage, we got into line to be processed through customs. After a while we noticed that everyone else in line, no matter whether they were Peruvians or foreigners, seemed to be getting through without any difficulty. We were the glaring exception and we were baffled.

Finally, an Alliance friend who already lived in Peru showed up at the dock to see what was the holdup. He chuckled at our naivete as he pulled out some Peruvian pounds, ran them through his fingers in an obvious motion and said to the customs agents: "Come on, fellows, what's wrong here? Let's get going." Seems that no one got through customs without virtually paying off the agents, because the government paid them a small salary and they were expected to make the rest of their living from such "tips."

Within ten minutes, we were cleared. The amazing thing was that none of our baggage—and there was a lot of it!—was opened. So Latin American Lesson Number One became: Sometimes I can't do things the "evangelical way"; I may have to literally buy my way.

We climbed on a streetcar and lumbered through the winding streets to a boarding house in the heart of Lima. Our rooms there were quite spacious, each opening onto a large patio. This gracious home was to be the site of a month and a half of intensive language training with a hired teacher.

Life in Lima was enjoyable. Our social life centered around the Methodist Girls' High School, where, as the only single male missionaries in the area, we became quite popular with the single women teachers. They invited us for tea and other activities. In fact, we soon realized that by spending so much time with other English-speaking people, we were losing opportunities to use our Spanish. Our habits had to change!

It would be more than a year before we traveled with equipment and supplies to actually set up our mission and begin our work of evangelizing the Campa Indians, but we knew we needed to scout the territory well in advance. So in July we set out on our first journey to select the spot where we would erect our buildings. The trip turned out to be more than we bargained for.

The Central Andean Railway of Peru, which at that time was the highest (in altitude) standard gauge railway in the world, was an engineering feat like nothing I had ever seen. The trip through breathtaking scenery included about

twenty-five switchbacks zigzagging through can-
yons—each bringing us to higher ground—plus
at least thirty tunnels.

Waiting for us on the other side of the
mountains was the town of Oroya, home to a
copper smelter and its workers. From Oroya
the railroad branched off in two directions.
We took the high road, arriving in Cerro de
Pasco, elevation 14,400 feet, the end of the
line and also the site of the copper mine
which supplied ore for Oroya, in late afternoon. The air was a bit rare and caused us
breathing difficulties.

From there we contracted a car and took a
very steep road that dropped approximately
7,000 feet to Huánuco. We killed the better
part of our first day in Huánuco contracting
with a man who made a business of taking people over the remainder of the mountains and
into the jungle by mule team. The next day we
started out early with two pack mules, three
saddle mules for us and two guides on foot.
The magnificent Central Andean Range
stretched out in front of us.

This part of the trip turned out to be more of
an adventure than we expected. For one thing,
we often became so sore that we would dis-
mount and walk rather than ride the mules.
Other times, we would climb down from our
animals at places so precarious we were sure
that if our mules went over the cliff we would
tumble down with them. Amazingly, whatever

the width of the trail, our surefooted guides kept the same steady, brisk pace.

When we got back up to about 10,000 feet, we ran into a rainstorm that quickly turned into an ice storm. Soon we were traveling a trail that was glazed over with ice. It appeared to be incredibly dangerous, but our guides didn't slow up a bit. Also, the mules didn't seem bothered by the slippery conditions; they would squeeze through any tight gap and traverse any narrow trail hugging a cliff.

By about 14,000 feet it became uncomfortably apparent to us that we were not going to make it over the mountains before dark. Our guides informed us that a big cave ahead would provide shelter, so we headed in that direction. When we arrived, we missionaries huddled inside while the guides unsaddled the mules, unloaded the baggage and stacked it all at the mouth of the cave before backing in themselves.

The air was extremely thin, so we didn't get much sleep. The next morning we layered on all the outfits we had brought (we had not been heavily clothed for the trip, because we were on our way to the tropics) and started out at dawn to head over the crest of the range.

It was beautiful sunny day. We reached the snow-capped pass at about 15,500 feet and gazed below to the trail dropping off rapidly toward the jungle. Directly below us was the mouth of an extinct volcano filled with crystal-clear water forming a sparkling lake. It shone like a jewel in the morning sun.

Our descent led us past the volcano and by dark we were down to about 2,000 feet. That night we took out our ponchos, stretched them over branches to form little tents and slept on the trail, being the only cleared area. This was the tail end of the rainy season, so everything was dripping wet. We were glad we had already acquired mosquito nets!

The next day we traveled deeper into the jungles, reaching a couple of settlements. One was inhabited by the Amuexia Indians, a friendly and semicivilized tribe who had been helpful to Peruvian settlers. They welcomed us into their dwellings but we slept in our own sleeping bags. The next day, we followed a river for about fifteen miles, often wading up to our hips in the thirty-three times we crossed it in an effort to follow a trail in the thick jungle.

Late that afternoon we arrived at Puerto Chuchuras, a Swiss settlement nestled on a cleared jungle plot. The Swiss had built wooden houses out of planks they sawed themselves and roofed them with handmade shingles—a rarity in the jungle. These people were living much like they had in Europe although they were deep in the heart of Peru.

We stayed overnight and began to dicker with the locals the next morning about taking us downriver in their canoes. It would be more than a day's travel to a junction with the Pichis

River where we would turn south and go upstream for several more days in search of a location for our station.

Finally we came to an agreement. We slept on sandbars along the river, taking advantage of the isolated white sandy banks away from army ants and other pesky insects. Fortunately, the rainy season was now over.

We paddled into an area where there were no other settlers. The Campa Indians were to the east. We found a high plateau which we reasoned had good protection from floods and excellent rain drainage. We discovered a little kink in the river with some large rocks forming a sort of natural port for tying up the canoes. So we pulled in for our first docking.

On shore we chopped our way through the bush and found a large level area several hundred yards long about the size of three or four city blocks. We could picture ourselves living here and beginning our ministry to the savage Campas.

After praying about it at length, we decided the Lord wanted us to claim this spot.

7

The Hole in the Wall

With the site chosen, we returned to Lima to resume our studies. But after a few weeks of book learning, we became restless to return to the interior. Our first taste of that wilderness had only made us hungry for more experiences with the native Peruvians, and we knew life would be the best teacher. This time we headed out in separate directions.

I wound up in Concepción, an inter-Andean market town. During my first week there I was invited to preach my first sermon in Español. They requested a sermon at least forty-five minutes in length, the customary time for people to consider a trip to church a worthwhile investment of their time. I worked on my sermon for hours, timing it and re-timing it. Finally, I figured I had enough material to last about thirty minutes and even this stretched my knowledge of Spanish almost to the limit. On the appointed day, I stepped up to the pulpit and preached my heart out, repeating the main points to draw out the time. Admittedly, I was nervous.

When I stepped down, I checked my watch. *Only twenty minutes! How could this be?* It was a humorous—and humbling—experience for a young man barely twenty-one years old. Years later I could still quote every word of that sermon.

I was assisting a Señor Guerrero, a native evangelist who was not highly trained but had an active ministry. Señor Guerrero and I would take all-day trips up and down the valley, sometimes riding trains and often just walking the roads, always selling Bibles. When the local Catholic priest would hear that we had been through his town, he would frequently follow in our footsteps, gathering up all the books we had sold and burning them. It's a far cry from what the Roman Catholic Church does today by distributing hundreds of thousands of copies of Scriptures, but this was the 1920s, and this established church felt threatened by our presence.

I began learning about the Indian way of life, sleeping in the wild and eating foods such as guinea pig which certainly had never been a part of my diet before. I also learned a disturbing reality of life: You can't live in Peru for long without getting body lice!

At first I didn't know what "they" were, other than realizing something was making me very miserable. And the lack of bathrooms—or any other way to take a bath—didn't help. The Indians seemed impervious to the discomfort but in the towns where Señor Guerrero and I stayed I usually made special arrangements with the lady of the house as soon as we arrived.

I would request that she heat a big pot of water and then stay clear of the patio around which her house was built. If it were a warm day with the sun shining on the patio, I could get a pretty good bath in privacy. These little mutual agreements resulted in my getting about one bath a week. That also became the time to get rid of the accumulation of body lice.

My biggest problem, however, was that the altitude was upsetting my digestive system. I eventually developed acosa diarrhea. There was no cure for it, so, because it was so debilitating after suffering for a period of time, I would have to go to a lower altitude to stop the diarrhea.

Some months after my work with Señor Guerrero and about a year after we had first set foot in Peru, Ray, Ben and I returned to Huánuco. This was the town we had visited on our first expedition into the jungle to select our eventual mission site. Charlie, who by now had finished his training at Nyack and arrived in Peru, at first stayed behind in Lima to continue with his language lessons. Later he joined us in Huánuco, and Ray returned to Lima.

We wanted to establish a church in this old colonial city high in the mountains, with its narrow, winding streets where llamas wandered freely. Soon after our arrival we rented a traditional-style Spanish house surrounded by a huge wall with a grand wooden front door that would open up to about ten feet wide. Cut into the door was a smaller door. We would leave the big door barred shut and use the smaller door for everyday coming and going.

As we became known around town, we learned that there was a bit of controversy associated with the house we had rented. Seems its owner was a successful businessman who owned one of the largest dairies in the area and thus had much influence. After a falling out with the local bishop, he rented the house to the Protestant missionaries to spite the bishop.

One day we heard loud banging on our big door. I went out and found that the source of the racket was an elderly Indian couple. They asked me in somewhat broken Spanish for a Bible. They said they lived over another mountain range and that their walk to our house had taken about seven hours. They cultivated coca leaves for a living, a popular product among Indians because it was the basis for cocaine. Although the drug could be extracted from the leaves through a fairly sophisticated production process on a bigger scale, the Indians had developed their own primitive process. They would mix the leaves with lime, chew the mixture and achieve a mild form of sedation. Apparently at one time this couple had been hooked on the drug themselves in addition to living off whatever profits their harvest would produce. And they had been alcoholics as well. But that was all in their past.

Once, while traveling to their distributor with a load of coca leaves, the husband had gotten drunk. In this vulnerable state, he was robbed. When he came to, he discovered that everything had been snatched from his inebriated body except a small book he found in his pocket. Unfortunately, he had been so drunk on rum that he couldn't remember how he had acquired the book earlier in the day. But being superstitious, he took it home and felt compelled to learn to read it. The book turned out to be a copy of the New Testament printed in Spanish.

There were only a few people in his town who could read, so he hounded them constantly to explain the letters and words. Slowly but surely, he learned to read it. In fact, he told us it would take so long for him to read a verse of Scripture that by the time he made it through the verse he had it memorized. Eventually he committed immense sections of the New Testament to memory.

Over a period of time this old man found Jesus Christ as his Savior by reading the New Testament. His wife and their three sons and their wives had formed a little church and were reading the book together. But it was risky business. Whenever they finished reading their New Testament, they would carefully tuck it into a small hole in the wall of their house and then cover the hole with a brick.

When word got out that they had this special book, the village priest came by to pick it up and burn it. He virtually ransacked their house, but they never told him where the book was hidden. Each member of the family made sure not to glance in the direction of the hole in the wall while the priest searched in what he thought was every nook and cranny. This scene was repeated several times.

After they heard we were in the area and had copies of what they understood to be a new book, they became bolder. *If this new book is as wonderful as the one we have, we want it,* they thought. They had walked the seven hours to our house in search of the "new" book.

At the end of their lengthy story, they showed us the worn and tattered book. We told them that, yes, we had a book, but it was the whole Bible, not just the New Testament. Until then they had no idea that what they had been reading so diligently in secret was only part of a larger book.

When we produced a copy for them, the wife grabbed it and hugged it and kissed it. The husband reverently looked through it, beginning in Genesis and turning page after page. Then suddenly, they seemed anxious to leave. Waving goodbye as they started back on their seven-hour walk, we promised to get over to their side of the mountain range for a visit to their little family church. Of course, we were thinking in terms of weeks.

Two days later came another big pounding on our door. We opened it and were startled to find their three sons.

"What do you mean sending our parents back with only one Bible? Didn't they tell you there are four families of us?" They wanted a complete Bible for each family. The seven-hour walk hadn't bothered them a bit. As we came to understand their culture, we realized this behavior was indicative of how hungry these people were for God's Word.

Later we learned there were twenty-eight Christians in their area of Chagua, and a thriving church which was started by this dear elderly couple.

> Opportunity! Opportunity! Opportunity! In no other way can we express the impression made upon us as we viewed the situation in Huánuco and the surrounding areas. "Behold an effectual door is opened." Well may these words be written today of the Alliance

work in the Huánuco sector. In a country where one finds rabid fanaticism, gross spiritual and intellectual darkness, mingled with a spirit of total indifference to things spiritual, among those who have broken away from the dominion of a corrupt priesthood, to see the Alliance hall in Huánuco crowded every night for two weeks with anywhere from 100 to 150 men and women made one's heart thrill. The earnest, intent faces of those who listened, without any restlessness, to what must have been to them long addresses, and who came back, night after night, for the series of meetings clearly indicated the hunger in their hearts for the things of God.

Oscar Lord
The Alliance Weekly
December 31, 1927

8

Homesteading in the Jungle

After our return from Huánuco we began gathering our equipment and supplies. We were finally ready to set up our mission camp in the jungle.

Unfortunately, however, only three of us would make this long-awaited journey. By now Charlie Marstaller had joined us, and everyone in our crew had been sick with one serious disease or another. All of us had a sort of "walking scarlet fever" which we finally diagnosed when large sheets of skin began peeling off our bodies. Ben Barton was the sickest of all.

We determined that Ben, who had been coughing for several months, had contracted tuberculosis. We packed this dear friend and fellow missionary off to New York, hoping for a recovery that never happened. He hemorrhaged several times on the voyage and lasted only a few days after arriving in New York's harbor. Only the Lord knows why Ben's death was permitted just as we were about to embark on our work.

It took us about six weeks to round up all we needed for life in the jungle. For example, money had no value there, so we needed trinkets (guns, ammunition, cooking utensils, knives) to trade with the Indians in exchange for work. We needed tools to clear a space in the dense undergrowth for our station. We needed enough food supplies to get us started until we could begin hunting, growing our own vegetables or otherwise living off of the land.

Ray Clark arranged for several Inca Indians from the middle highlands to clear the land—only a half acre or so at first—and to build a small hut. It was to be about twelve feet by eighteen feet and would be our living quarters until we could construct a more permanent building.

Ray had confidence in the Incas. They were products of one of the world's greatest ancient civilizations, the famous Inca Empire whose ancestors trace their history back to the first century after Christ. Inca engineers had built roads, bridges, irrigations systems and aqueducts that united the ancient kingdom which at its apex stretched from southern Colombia to

northern Argentina. In 1531, when the Incas
were at the height of their glory as an empire,
the Inca capital of Cuzco was conquered by
Francisco Pizarro and his men, who were
driven by their greed for gold. Pizarro founded
the city of Lima in 1535 and it became the
capital for Spanish viceroys. Peru was the last
of the South American countries to throw off
the yoke of Spain. The final battle for liberation
was fought in 1824.

In the last century the new nation had fought
numerous battles with its neighboring South
American countries. But the Incas, who in the
meantime had retreated to the irrigated high-
land valleys, were still known for their progres-
sive ways and engineering skills. I felt secure
knowing that people of this caliber were preparing a way for us. Many of the other Peruvian Indians were characterized by the Alliance
as "savage or semi-savage." One tribe was still
cannibalistic and most tribes had no known
history of civilization, including the Campas in
whose territory we would be homesteading.

We left Lima on Friday the 13th of August,
1926. Horses and mules were loaded with the
three of us plus our equipment and supplies for
the six-day trip inland to the exotic-sounding
town of Puerto Bermudez. There we would
start downriver for the final three-day leg of
our journey. We took only two saddle animals
on the theory that each of us would become

too saddle sore if we rode the entire way. We traveled about ten hours a day, swapping off riding and walking.

The trail was four or five feet wide, sometimes a few inches less on ledges where we guided our animals around the faces of cliffs. We forded seven or eight rivers. With no bridges over these jungle waterways, we unloaded our pack animals and moved the gear across each river by canoe as the animals swam to the other side. Then we loaded them up again and continued along the obscure trail through towering trees and thick underbrush.

At night we slept in government-built *tambos*—palm-thatched huts with walls made of split palm wood. The government had also strung a one-line telephone system through which, with strong enough lungs, we could yell over to determine from one *tambo* to the next who and how many were coming.

At Puerto Bermudez we purchased a large canoe and headed down the Pichis River. It wasn't much work going down because the current ran about three miles an hour. Most of our paddling was to guide the heavily loaded craft. At night we camped on sandy banks along the river. We arrived at Cahuapanas on August 22, ready to begin our work.

Two Inca Indians greeted us there and helped us haul ashore our supplies. We inspected the little dirt-floor hut they had built for us. We also paced the 600 acres assigned to our team on the condition that we could not learn the Campa language. This tract had been the result of our best negotiations with the current government regime. We weren't satisfied with agreeing to the language limitation in exchange for the land, but it was the best deal we could negotiate given the political climate.

The president of Peru, who had taken over the government in a revolutionary coup, was extremely anti-Roman Catholic and anticlerical. He was happy to approve any measures he thought would inhibit and/or frustrate efforts of the established church. So when we approached him for permission to settle in this area of his country, he granted it. He insisted, however, that we teach Spanish to the Campa Indians and attempt to make Peruvian citizens out of them. This condition handicapped our work somewhat, but we couldn't risk being thrown out of the country by a blood-thirsty dictator. So we followed orders. (In later years, missionaries continuing the work begun on these original 600 acres have been allowed to learn the Campa language and today this tribe has the Bible in their language, translated by Wycliffe Bible Translators.)

We came ashore and set up our campsite with three distinct goals. The first, which we shared with all Alliance missionaries, was to glorify God with our lives and to live for Him. The second was simply to survive. White men had never gone into this area and returned alive after contact with the savage Campas. Our third aim was to win these people to Christ and to start a church among them.

Even in the wilds of South America I felt it was important for me to identify and verbalize my goals in order to be focused and, hopefully, successful. What I soon realized was that the goal of staying alive would be a great deal harder to achieve than it sounded.

It took us several months to settle into our new lives. Days were filled with the strenuous, exhausting work of carving out a bare existence for humans on a hostile piece of land that had been the private territory of monkeys, wild boars and many other species suited for life among gigantic trees and an undergrowth so thick I could barely see daylight through it.

At night all of us went into the temporary hut and fell bone-tired into hammocks covered with mosquito nets. The mosquitos in that dark, damp climate were what I called man-sized and, along with the pesky vampire bats, were a constant annoyance. The Inca helpers stayed on for a while, but sharing the little hut for cooking and sleeping among so many men was a bit too close for comfort.

I also had to cope with homesickness. The mail launch, a forty-foot-long canoe that floated right past our hut, was a welcome sight to a man in his early twenties for whom the deserts of Arizona seemed like a fading dream. The trouble was that the launch arrived only about twice a month.

The river was our link to the civilized world in other ways too. We bought food from people paddling by in their canoes. Occasionally we ordered supplies from the United States that arrived via this vital waterway. A big occasion was to unload, for example, a five-gallon tin of pork fat or maybe a 100-pound bag of beans. We unpacked our new purchases with a lot of pomp and flourish, often celebrating with a special meal prepared with food from the latest shipment. Mostly, though, we purchased roots and seeds to plant our own food.

We spent several weeks of backbreaking labor to clear small parcels of land to support even the minimum of growth. Trees were five to six feet in diameter and their root systems spread fifty to sixty feet under a sweeping canopy of branches and leaves. In addition, the underbrush was dense. We had to clear all this and more to open up areas allowing enough sunlight to reach our delicate new plants. It was us against the elements! For weeks I sawed and hacked as sore muscles became well developed muscles. Finally felling a huge tree gave me a hard-earned feeling of achievement.

The land was fertile with humus. But our area got several hundred inches of rain each year which would soon wash away the rich soil we had exposed to sunlight and, of course, a direct pelting of rainwater. So during the years we farmed this territory we didn't dare use any one acre of land for long. This meant constantly rotating the crops to intentionally allow the abandoned fields to become overgrown again. It was an exhausting process, but I felt a sense of accomplishment when fresh young plants poked through the new fields we created.

In the beginning, we had no chickens or animals so all our meat came out of the jungle. Our nearest neighbors were a couple of families of semicivilized Indians who lived in their huts about an hour and a half downstream from us. They taught us how to hunt for birds such as partridges or meaty animals like deer or wild hogs. The Indians, dressed in loose fitting handwoven gowns dyed with tree sap, were easily camouflaged among the mostly brown shades of the jungle. They were clever at imitating almost any sound. Their method was to squat among the bushes and then call their prey. These forays into the jungle armed with shotguns usually produced some good eating but our meat meals were strictly feast or famine. With no refrigeration, all we could do was skin our kill, cut it into strips and either smoke or roast as much of it as we thought we could eat. Between hunts, our diet was mostly beans, rice and the local cooking bananas called plantains.

We also caught fish. I envied the method perfected by the Indians, who could spot a fish under the surface and get off a successful bow and arrow shot at least half the time. Because their arrows had long stems of hollow reed, the pierced fish would drift up to the water's surface where the Indian hunters simply gathered them up by hand.

So these were our main sources of food. Eventually, we arranged to have canned goods and staples such as butter, flour and baking powder shipped to us from the States. It took several months for our first shipment to reach us.

We planned to take turns cooking, but somehow the job usually landed on me, the youngest. After our diet became a bit more varied and our menu more interesting, I found an advantage to often winding up with this task: I could cook what I wanted.

We also adjusted to the rain. Some days we would get soaked to the bone, but we hated to quit working and got to where we paid little attention to a downpour. It cooled us off, and the wet didn't seem to hurt us. Trouble was, mosquitos inevitably followed the rain, and we often came down with the malaria they carried.

Occasionally an Indian or two lived with us in those early months. If he was lazy and hardly worth his food, we would send him back home. But even Indians that weren't particularly ambitious were good company.

I learned what loneliness was down there in that enormous jungle. We missionaries had each other, and we had the Lord. We did a lot of singing and maybe sometimes even talked to ourselves!

The following is excerpted from an article entitled "Jungle Life at Cahuapanas, Peru," written by Ray Clark, *The Alliance Weekly*, Feb. 12, 1927:

At about 5:30 in the morning I turned in my hammock, rubbed my eyes, stretched myself and looked around to see what had awakened me. The morning air had a decided chill in it, and a light mist was rising from the river as the first indications of the dawn appeared in the east. From across the river there came the weird sounds of a "howling" monkey, and already some of the larger birds were to be heard, including our five hens and the rooster who were just coming out of their wonderfully crude-looking shelter, ready once again to make war on the multitudes of ants that form their chief article of diet.

One by one we crawled out, some from their hammocks, others off their hard palm wood beds. "Dressing" is an easy operation on the Pichis. No collars or ties to adjust, no shaving, no shoes to shine or clothes to be brushed! All is as easy as rolling off the proverbial log and takes but a few minutes! It was not surprising, then, that we were all ready by the time our meal was spread.

How inviting it sounds to write of a hot

morning meal being spread! To eat the meal that actually was spread was not nearly so inviting. Six plates in two rows, one on either side of the palm wood bed from which our cook had just risen. In the center of the bed, placed on a greasy-looking board which once formed the top of a kerosene case, was a large black kettle in which there was a portion of warmed-over rice from the previous day.

Alongside of this was a frying pan piled with fried yucca flour, and in our respective mugs there was coffee or hot water, according to taste. Our coffee beans were crushed on a flat root of a large tree with a suitable rounded stone. Needless to say the coffee had a very unusual coffee flavor and large lumps floated around the edges to remind us of the need of a coffee mill. When we were especially fortunate we had molasses with which to sweeten this drink.

On more than one occasion our food supplies were reduced to next to nothing. Once the supply of yucca flour, rice, lard and molasses had completely run out before our supplies which had been ordered from the Chuchuras Colony—four days away by canoe—had arrived, and we were reduced to a plantain diet, and even these were almost gone! Of course there is always game in the jungle, but our inexperience in the ways of hunting in the woods made this a rather uncertain source of supply.

Whenever we could secure an Indian to hunt for us he would usually return with a bird of some kind, or a monkey, or a wild hog. We, however, had found it hard to secure the aid of Indians for this purpose, they themselves having their own families to feed and their own cultivations to work.

This does not mean that we were never successful. Clyde Taylor, our most successful hunter, often came to the rescue. We have eaten many varieties of fish, flesh and fowl, including various large birds, as well as parrots, and even owls! Among the animals eaten were wild pig, deer, monkey and sloth, the nicest of these being the pork and the monkey meat. Fish, turtles and turtles' eggs have also helped to make our meals more savory. On one occasion we were reduced to nothing but red beans, which we ate three times a day, and we were glad when we obtained a new supply of plantains, and still more happy when a canoe load from Chuchuras arrived with more yucca flour, molasses and rice. Our food problem at first was one of great difficulty and we are now glad to report that supplies of such things as flour, condensed milk, canned meats, etc., reach us regularly from Iquitos, 1,000 miles downstream, and we look forward to the coming springtime when we hope to reap our own harvest of rice, corn, yucca and plantains, as well as such things as beans and other vegetables.

9

Angels on the Roof

He arrived one day while we were building our permanent station, the one we called "the big house."

Majestically he strode ashore adorned in full Campa regalia of multi-colored beads and an elaborate feathered crown topping a head that already towered several inches above his two companions. They were dressed in simple blue pants and shirts.

The trio arrived in a canoe large enough to hold at least twenty Indians but, after a surreptitious inspection, we concluded that only these men had been aboard. We wanted to be hospitable, but we certainly couldn't throw caution to the wind. The Campas were savages.

The leader spoke minimal Spanish, so we communicated with our few common words and sign language. We offered him food which he rejected. He did not go into our hut, but I observed that he took note of the big house we were constructing. With his brightly painted skin and enormous feathered headdress it was obvious he was dressed to impress us with his longstanding control of the area.

The premise of the visit was to sell us two parrots. We obliged and paid for the birds with five yards of red calico. We brought out our Victrola and played a record for him. The old hand-cranked machine produced scratchy music, yet it seemed to fascinate him. He circled it slowly, almost reverently, peering at it from every angle with a look of amusement, perhaps even joy on his face. I was relieved to see a human reaction out of this potentially violent man. He was checking us out, probably thinking: *What are these foreigners up to? Are they a threat to my control and presence? Should I consider killing them? Do they have anything worth stealing?*

Just as abruptly as he appeared on our riverbank he suddenly said *adios* and left. Later we learned from the few families we had befriended that our mysterious visitor was the Campa tribal chief. We hoped we had made the right impression on this powerful warrior who often boasted that he had murdered six white men.

The significance of his visit became clear a few weeks later. Finishing up our work late one afternoon we noticed a full moon just above the horizon. Dusk settled on the jungle within minutes but the enormous white ball in the sky sprinkled light among the towering trees.

A canoe silently cut through the water heading downstream. One lone Campa paddled the enormous craft, a clue to us that other Indians were nearby, possibly ashore. Although one Indian could steer such a large canoe moving with the current, we knew that six or eight strong-armed men were required to paddle and control it on the upstream journey. And these were only the crew. Another fifteen to twenty could ride as passengers.

Where are all those Indians? I wondered as I set down my hoe. A chill went up my spine as it dawned on me that they could be hiding among the trees all around us.

Before long, we knew they were.

An eerie series of whistles pierced the silence. These were signals—a complicated conversation, really—created by whistling through cupped hands over mouths or by blowing through large snail shells. The calls carried for nearly half a mile aided by the still night air and the surface of the water.

We had been told that if the Campas ever attacked us it would be at night and during a full moon. We had been apprised of their technique for robbing—and perhaps murdering—us. The Indians were remarkably accurate with a bow and arrow, a skill I admired when used for spearing a rapidly swimming fish but which gave me more than the shudders when I realized it might be used for our demise. Their custom was to scrape a bark they found to be flammable, tie it onto the points of their deadly arrows and light it with a torch. Then they shot these flaming arrows high into the air at an arc calculated to pierce the thatched roof of their prey's hut. As soon as it caught fire they would rush in, grab anything of value and dash out again. The fire they had begun overhead served as light for their thievery and a cover-up for their crime by burning down the hut. If the hut's inhabitants happened to be asleep or otherwise caught unawares when the attack began, as often as not these pagan warriors would kill them.

The three of us quickly surmised this was in store for us. We left everything behind except rifles, shotguns and flashlights and headed into the jungle, huddling together just out of sight of our hut but close enough to hear the whistle signals. Swatting at the hordes of mosquitoes, we spent the night worrying about the vicious and nocturnal army ants and praying fervently for God to intervene in this potentially deadly situation.

The whistles continued a while. Then, around midnight, they intensified and we could see the warriors gathering around our hut. Suddenly, silence. Inexplicably, the Indians retreated to the water's edge, boarded their huge canoe and paddled quickly away.

We came out from our hiding place about daybreak. The hut was standing just as we had left it. Cautiously we poked through all our belongings and found everything intact. Other than obscure traces of our uninvited visitors' stealthy encroachment and sudden retreat, nothing seemed disturbed. We picked up our implements and went about our lives as usual.

Several years later we learned what had happened on that moonlit night. The tribal chief who had visited us wearing his impressive but flamboyant costume became one of our converts. He named himself Elias, Spanish for Elijah. After his conversion he depended on Christ rather than the idols he had worshiped in the past or the brute strength of his people to provide his security. And, like men of any culture whose hearts are softened by the Holy Spirit (no matter that they aren't knowledgeable about the details of Christian theology), he became willing to share his vulnerabilities.

Questioned about that night, Elias lowered his head, looked down at the ground and finally admitted, "Yes, we did come to attack you."

Asked how many warriors he brought, he replied, "Quite a few." He then grouped his fingers together with some of his comrades to indicate that the number was somewhere between thirty and forty Indians. We had been outnumbered ten to one!

Asked why they retreated, why they didn't follow through with their plans to attack us, he said, "We were afraid to. There were too many of you."

Bewildered, the missionaries questioned him further.

"Your roof was covered with white people all wearing white *cushmas*," Elias explained. *Cushmas* were the traditional sack-like gowns worn by the Indians. Theirs were brown. He described the *cushmas* worn by our "warriors" as dazzling white.

"We were afraid to go near the hut because we knew we didn't stand a chance against such an impressive army."

Apparently, God does send His angels now and again to protect His own. From then on, we felt perfectly safe. In fact, we never again abandoned the house in fear after dark.

Whenever Dad told this story I was struck by the fact that the angels completely covered the roof. There wasn't space for even one arrow to pierce the thatch!

It taught me that whatever the Lord provides, He provides in abundance. Also, He provides exactly what communicates most effectively to the people He's reaching. In this case, His angels were dressed in gowns like the cushmas *worn by the Indians. The Lord always appears to us in a way we can understand.*

My daughter has used this story many times to witness to friends.

Carolyn Taylor Thompson
Oveido, Florida

L to R: Charles Marstaller, Clyde Taylor, Ben Barton and Ray Clark (seated) begin their journey of a lifetime. Taken in Jamaica, 1924. Clyde was only 19 years of age, the youngest missionary ever to be sent overseas by The Christian and Missionary Alliance.

The Marstaller family of Durham, Maine, 1922. L to R back row: Len, *Esther*, *David*, August, Anna, *Charles*, Martha.
L to R front row: *Ruth*, *Louisa*, Barney, Emma, Wilhelm, *Betty*, Lydia.
Those whose names appear in italics all attended the Missionary Training Institute (now Nyack College), in Nyack, New York.

L to R: Charles, Clyde and Ray as they appeared in Peru. These costumes are still owned by the family.

Two Campa Indian families live in each house with sparse furnishings and palm platforms for beds.

Guerrero and Clyde arrive at their destination looking somewhat rumpled. "It's useless to . . . dress up," Clyde noted. "With rain and the like, it would ruin decent clothes."

The "Big House." It seemed like a mansion to the men. The foundation and main structure was made of ebony and is still standing. The station is now operated by the South American Indian Mission.

Llamas usually live above 8,000 feet. This picture was taken near the high Andes town of Huancayo.

"One of two views that I took of a marriage celebration. Most everybody was drunk. The old fellow with the mask, the master of ceremonies, was good and drunk." Clyde

"This is the village that turned almost entirely to the gospel when they heard it. They forbid the priest to come to the village." Clyde

"Ourselves and our house. The mosquito net with the typewriter on trunk below is where I was writing letters." Clyde

"This is the picture of me typing the diary. I look almost all legs and feet. Taken in front of the door to my room in the patio in Huánuco." Clyde

Clyde and Ruth on their wedding day, June 7, 1930. The maid of honor is Ruth's sister, Betty Marstaller; best man is Merrill C. Tenney. All four were graduates of the Missionary Training Institute.

The students and faculty pose after construction is completed at the Bible Institute in Armenia, Colombia.

Clyde and Ruth, right of center, with the 1939 faculty and student body.

Clyde officiates at a baptismal service in the Quindio River at Armenia.

The Alliance congregation in Armenia.

The 1937 field conference of Alliance missionaries in Colombia; George Constance on left, Helen next to him. Across from him, beginning in the foreground is Cora Murdock Zook, Betty Marstaller, Elsie Bauman, Madge Miller, Della Smith.

Orletta enjoys a bicycle ride with Daddy.

The Bible Institute in Armenia.

The first graduates of the Institute. L to R: Ernesto Martinéz, Ramón Lopez, Josué Leal.

Field conference, 1940. L to R back row: Clyde Taylor, Betty Marstaller,
Leo Tennies, Emmanuel Prentice, Fred Smith, Wes Perry,
Elsie Rupp Bauman, George Constance.
L to R front row: Clyde Donald Taylor, Ruth Taylor, Madge Miller,
Ruth Tennies with Winston, Edna Prentice, Della Smith with Helen,
Amy Perry, Helen Constance with David and George Jr.

Major General Charles Carpenter seen with Clyde just before leaving for an 8,000 mile survey trip to Arctic air bases, March 14, 1957.

Clyde receives his master's degree at Boston University, 1942. Sister-in-law, Betty Marstaller on the left; Ruth on the right.

Dr. Louis L. King, president of The Christian and Missionary Alliance, presides at the final session of the Wheaton Congress, April 1966. Clyde is fourth from the right.

The Clyde Taylor family, 1974.
Back Row, L to R: Clyde Donald, Orletta (Gillikin), Darlene (Tate), Carolyn (Thompson).
Front Row: Clyde and Ruth.

Above, Clyde preached at the Young Hak Presbyterian Church in Seoul, Korea during a trip for World Relief.

Visting a Korean factory, part of a silk farm sponsored by World Relief to enable Korean nationals to earn an independent living.

Clyde and Ruth, taken at the time of Clyde's retirement from the National Association of Evangelicals, 1974.

Dr. Clyde W. Taylor, 1904 to 1988.

Dr. Taylor poses with President Nixon, Rev. Everett Graffam, head of World Relief, and Mrs. Nguyen Thi Khang (Gwen), supervisor and head nurse of the Hoa Khanh Children's Hospital in Vietnam. The President presented her with an Inaugural Medal for her care of almost 60,000 patients during the conflict. Taken April 22, 1970 in the Oval Office.

10

You Never Know Who's Watching

Our mission site was a beehive of construction activity during the first couple of months after we arrived in Cahuapanas. We arranged for some Swiss men we had met on our scouting visit the previous year to come over from their village about three canoe-days away. We needed their axes, steel wedges, semi-round chisels plus their knowledge of building solid structures out of the jungle's natural resources. With the addition of some hired Indians, this cross-cultural crew began building the big house.

Because of my construction experience back home in Phoenix, I took to this task with relish. I enjoyed the challenge of erecting a building

using towering palm trees, thin but sturdy saplings, thick vines and even leaves. It was gratifying to use my boyhood training in this dark,
remote jungle and to learn new skills from people who could transform an overgrown forest
we could barely walk through into a civilized
and functional mission station. Also, I felt secure realizing that God had planted all the
building materials we needed in this dense
thicket where saplings and parasitic vines
found as much nourishing sunlight as mature
trees reaching 120 feet into the air.

The best building materials on hand were
huge palm trees twelve inches in diameter by
forty feet high. These were ideal for fashioning
into wallboards and floorboards because of
their flexibility and strength. Without planing
tools, we had to improvise using other construction methods. The Swiss taught us how to
fell the palms, saw them into six-foot lengths,
crack them open with wedges and cut out their
fleshy interiors with semi-round chisels. This
process reduced their bulk which allowed us to
flatten out the remaining sections into a material resembling a lathed board about thirty
inches wide. Used as floors, these palm boards
were a bit springy, so we reinforced them with
joists made of smaller palms which we left intact. These saplings also became our wall posts
and rafters for the roof. Palm leaves were laid
on top as thatch. So every size of palm tree and
every portion of this valuable jungle conifer

was used for the big house which measured eighteen feet wide by thirty feet long. The framework was reinforced with an intricate weaving of vines, another material we had in great supply.

The addition of the roof for the big house was a lesson in humility as a result of not paying attention to local common sense a few months earlier when we added a thatch roof to our original hut. We had been told that if we didn't cut the palm leaves at the right time according to the moon's cycle the crickets would eat them. We thought that was nonsense. So we cut the leaves and covered our rafters with them according to our own schedule. Well, we were wrong. Millions of crickets had a feast at our expense, literally eating the roof off the building.

We didn't make this mistake on the big house. Not only were the leaves cut at the proper time but we also piled them extra thick. Of course, this did not keep the insects out of our mission house—they were free to come and go as they pleased through the open windows and the cracks in the floor—but the extra thick roof did keep out the rain.

The finishing touch was to add permanent front steps leading up to the door. The house was set on sturdy stilts about six feet above the ground. This kept out all but the most adventurous snakes and made the house cooler for sleeping. Our beds for the big house were also an improvement over the flimsy hammocks we had been using. We fashioned them with wooden frames made of the same palm wood as the house, plus thin mattresses. Of course, we used mosquito nets. However, we continued to take our afternoon *siestas* in hammocks.

We finally settled in, gathered around our stove shipped to us from New York and started a roaring fire. As a reminder that all our needs would be provided, we discovered that Amazon jungle wood is wonderful for burning. We had already learned that this heavy timber—unless carved out for a canoe—is too heavy to float. But the advantage to hard wood is that it's easy to split. We paid Indians to cut our firewood.

One night a few weeks after moving into the big house our dogs began to bark furiously. Hearing the ruckus, we jumped out of bed, pulled on our trousers, grabbed the ever-present rifle and headed out the door.

I half expected to see a jaguar prowling our yard. These huge cats measured eight feet nose to tail, had footprints eight inches across and weighed at least 200 pounds. Our dogs had sense enough not to tangle with them. Fortunately, jaguars were just as afraid of us as we were of them, but sometimes it took a gunshot or two to convince them that we were in the vicinity.

Another idea flashing through my mind as we braced ourselves for trouble was that a herd of wild boars had frightened the dogs. Anything was fair game to these vicious pigs—jaguars, snakes, even humans. The best defense against their attack was to shinny up the nearest tree. And fast! We had witnessed some mutilated carcasses gored to death by their razor sharp eight-inch tusks.

Whatever riled up the dogs must have retreated back into the jungle, I thought sleepily. Someone suggested we check our little makeshift port on the riverbank before heading back to bed. So we stumbled down the slope leading to the water's edge. We could hardly believe what we saw. There sat two Indian families who had been working for us but always returned at night to their own huts downstream. The two large canoes were overflowing with chickens, dogs, children and household goods.

One of the men was designated as the group's spokesman. He said simply, "We want to live with you." He added that they would be happy to set up housekeeping under the big house until they could build huts of their own.

We were flabbergasted and asked why they had made this decision. Their answer, communicated with sign language and the few common words we knew, surprised us. They pointed to a tree and told us they had watched us from that perch when we thought no one was looking. We gazed up at their hiding place and saw it provided a good view of our clearing as we went about our daily activities. It also concealed any view of the Indians with their camouflaged clothing.

Clever, I thought, wondering what eyes might be on us that very moment.

Miguel and Sancho struggled for the right words and signs to convey what we recognized to be our first successful Christian witness by action. In effect they said: "We decided to pull up our roots and relocate our families, so we could learn to live like you. We observe that you never beat your dogs. We notice that you never fight among yourselves. In fact, we see that you never even raise your voices in anger. We also like the respectful way you treat us. Every time we paddle by on the river you greet us cheerfully. You seem to be sincerely interested in us as human beings. And your word is good. We have hunted for you and done many other tasks at your request. You always pay us what you promise. And you pay us promptly."

Naturally, these weren't their exact words, but we got the message.

I was touched that these men were sensitive to our interactions, were hungry for what we knew to be gospel-inspired behavior and had the courage to admit that a better life was available. I respected them as husbands and fathers who accepted responsibility for leading their families away from the witchcraft-worshiping culture that must have been deeply ingrained in their lives.

It's a beginning, I told myself as I helped them carry their belongings up to the big house.

"The Indians are watching." That's become a code phrase in our family to remind us that you never know who's taking note of how you're behaving.

Dad told this story to a class I was teaching. The children were mesmerized. To think that people were up in the trees watching him and his fellow missionaries when they thought they were all alone! After that, all I had to do was murmur "the Indians are watching," if a child got out of line.

Darlene Taylor Tate
Annapolis, Maryland

11

Christmas in the Big House

We praise God for all that He has enabled us to do in the past months, but we are earnestly trusting that before very long we shall have the joy of seeing some of these sun-worshiping Campa Indians turning to God and accepting Jesus Christ as their Savior. This is our great objective. Please pray with us that those now on the station may comprehend the story of redeeming grace and accept the Savior.

Ray Clark
"Progress at Cahuapanas, Peru"
Excerpted from *The Alliance Weekly*
July 28, 1928

The Campa Indians were a religious people, if your definition of "religious" means being worshipers of a power you perceive to be higher than yourself. Trouble was, the Campas were animists. That is, they worshiped spirits, and I'm not referring to the Holy Spirit about whom they knew nothing in the 1920s when we three missionaries were opening up this territory for the Alliance. Instead, the Indians to whom we were assigned worshiped objects, and they worshiped spirits they believed inhabited these objects. And by "worship" I mean they feared these spirit-filled objects rather than loved them, depended on them or knew of any saving grace provided by them.

For example, a Campa could tell you what spirit lived in a certain rock or a certain tree. They might make wide circles around such a rock or tree if they believed it was inhabited by a spirit. They knew the personality of that spirit, what it would do *to* them if they crossed it or what it would do *for* them if they worshiped it in an acceptable way. So the Campas spent a lot of energy on worshiping objects.

We discovered that when the full moon came up they would get down on their knees in front of the moon and say something like: "Oh, moon. We worship you. And, if someone made you, we worship him who made you." This was encouraging to us missionaries because it meant they had no trouble believing in a Creator. In fact, we learned that they knew a rough version of the Noah's ark story, a tale of a man and his wife, children and animals aboard a big boat who survived a flood that killed everyone else. Where they got this story, we never did find out. But this discussion led to others and, despite the cumbersome language barrier between us and Sancho and Miguel and their families, we soon gathered that they had some understanding of the concepts of sin and themselves as sinners.

We decided we should explain to the two Indian families with whom we were now sharing our property why we had moved to the jungle. They seemed to realize we weren't there to begin a large profitable farm. They could see that we cleared only enough land and planted only enough crops for our own use. So the unspoken question became: *Why are you men here?*

Christmas was coming. This seemed like the natural opportunity to share what burned in our hearts and what we longed to tell them but knew they must hear only in stages and as the Holy Spirit led us.

We faced the problem all missionaries eventually face when opening up a new territory: how to relate the gospel to people who have no clue at all about the story or its significance. Our solution was to concentrate our Christmas celebration on the concept of gifts. We figured a Christmas tree would have no meaning to them. But we thought we could get our point across with gifts given to them after a hearty meal.

Gifts. Little did we know when we planned this get-together that we could not have chosen a theme that would be more confusing or emotionally loaded for these people! Fortunately, the Holy Spirit helped us communicate our idea.

Before they arrived for dinner we took the largest cardboard box we could find and filled it with gifts for them. We tied strings to each gift and draped the strings over the sides of the box. These were to represent fishing lines to make the after-dinner activity into a sort of "going fishing" game.

Our nine guests included the two sets of parents and their combined five children. They arrived at the appointed time and enjoyed our meal plus the music we played for them on our Victrola. We told them the traditional Christmas story about how Jesus came to earth as a baby and how He had been the Creator of all that they knew and worshiped—the sun, the moon, the stars and everything on earth. They listened with rapt attention, but because of the language barrier we weren't sure how much they really understood.

When we got to the part about how God's gift to humanity was the gift of His Son, we decided this would be better illustrated with the gifts we had prepared for them. We brought out the box with the strings hanging over the edge. Each family member "went fishing." Out came a small hand mirror for Sancho's wife. Another string produced cloth for the wife of Miguel. We showed her how she could make this into a dress for herself complete with slits for her arms and head as was their custom. Next came trousers for the men. At this point we noticed the first emotional reaction from any of them—it was not the reaction we expected. They seemed terribly disturbed! Miguel, the most communicative of the bunch, indicated that he did not want his trousers, which we knew would cost him the equivalent of about $1.50 or two weeks of work. Miguel, trying to explain his reaction with his limited Spanish vocabulary, finally gave up in frustration and just recoiled from the whole activity.

The three of us communicated among ourselves, mostly with eye contact and murmurs. Finally, it became clear that I should try to talk to Miguel. I approached him gingerly. The problem? Miguel wanted to know how much work he would have to do to earn his new trousers.

I answered, "No work, Miguel. The trousers are a *gift*." But Miguel didn't understand and continued to back away. In fact, he seemed ready to bolt from the whole scene. Naturally, this was putting quite a damper on our Christmas party.

After several more minutes of awkward communication I figured out what was the *real* problem. Although we were speaking Spanish, the word for "gift" had no meaning to these Campa Indians whose native language had no such word. This was an important revelation. Since language follows culture, the Campa culture knew nothing about the concept of receiving something without having to work for it.

What a leap in understanding, I thought to myself as I considered how I would persuade Miguel to rejoin our party so they could learn about God's gift to humanity. *If they don't understand about giving gifts to each other, how will we teach them about God's grace?*

I was still pondering this dilemma when, on the other side of the room, Miguel's daughter "went fishing" for her gift. The little girl pulled on her string and out of the cardboard box popped a celluloid doll about six inches tall.

The girl immediately let out a cry and dropped the doll to the floor. The other Indians gasped and all of them backed away, apparently in fear. Naturally, Miguel and I broke up what was passing for a private discussion and rejoined the group of petrified-looking Indians huddled in fear of this doll. As a social occasion, this party was going downhill fast!

We missionaries looked at one another and partly out of nervousness began to chuckle. The Indians glared at us, obviously not amused! This was serious stuff. Although my insides were erupting in laughter, I straightened up my face and concentrated on trying to figure out what was going on.

Finally Miguel reached into the circle with his foot and touched the doll with his toe. Quickly he withdrew it as if the doll could bite. I had to clasp my hands over my mouth to keep from laughing out loud.

Miguel did it again. And again. Naturally, the doll did not bite. One by one they began to realize the doll was not alive.

When their comfort level seemed higher, I picked up the doll and showed them that it was hollow. They drew in closer, fascinated that an object that looked so human was not human. Eventually Miguel took it in his own hands and examined it from every possible angle. He turned it over with extreme care as if it were a miniature human baby that he could bruise if he accidentally mishandled it.

Finally Miguel began to laugh, possibly the heartiest laughter I had ever heard, or so it seemed to one who was dying to laugh out loud himself. Then the whole party broke out in laughter, that universal language that is both a relief and a form of bonding. Our laughter lasted for several minutes—a great icebreaker for a party that was desperately in need of one.

We had touched these people and they had touched us.

We celebrated late into the night, eating more, hearing more music, enjoying the gifts and mostly talking about the gift of our Lord.

When they left, hugging and thanking us profusely, I believe they had some small insight into the meaning and significance of God's grace.

That evening was the beginning, I always felt, of our evangelizing the Campa Indians.

12

White Men versus the Elements

The next couple of years were filled with progress both in our work of evangelizing the Indians and improving the physical facility at Cahuapanas.

Sancho and Miguel and their families began attending a Bible study. Eventually they became our first Christian converts. Little by little word spread among their friends that these two families were worshiping one God—the one true God—instead of many gods. What seemed most impressive to other Campas was the nature of this new God. As the Holy Spirit enlightened the new converts, they began to understand the distinctions between fearing God in a respectful manner and fearing the many gods of their past experience who might do spiteful, even demonic, acts. A Swiss settler also joined the group which began meeting on Sunday mornings as well as for weekday Bible studies. With his addition we began breaking down the cultural barriers, the we/they concept that sometimes crops up on the mission field. The Indians began to understand that our God was for everyone, not just for American missionaries and Campa Indians. Their universe was expanding and so was their understanding of the greatness of God. It was a tremendous breakthrough.

The hunting and fishing trips with our new companions now took on new meaning in addition to bringing home food. Our goal was to reach people in areas even more remote than the Pichis River. We taught our new converts how to witness to their own people. Of course they weren't restricted by the language limitation laid on us by the president of Peru, so now the gospel could be spread in the Campa language.

We baptized many converts in those first couple of years. We also organized a church and started a grammar school. (Nearly fifty years later while working as executive secretary of the Evangelical Foreign Missions Association I hired a Wycliffe airplane to fly me up-river to Cahuapanas from Wycliffe's facility at the headwaters of the Amazon. I was thrilled to see that the Campa school system had

grown and expanded to higher grades and that
a medical clinic had been established. In subsequent years the Alliance work we began was
handed over to the South American Indian
Mission. I was especially pleased to learn that
the Campas had become highly respected citizens of the Peruvian government because of
their almost nonexistent crime rate and lack of
many other social ills. This proved to me that
the Lord's hand was working even when the
Peruvian dictator of the 1920s seemed to
handicap us with his requirement that we not
learn the Campa language in exchange for a
600-acre plot of land. As always, if the Lord
wants His message to spread, He overcomes
all obstacles.)

With our growing congregation came increasing demands. Now that we were on the Alliance map with converts and a population of
new Christians, we knew Cahuapanas would
become a significant mission station. Before
long missionaries would not be limited to single men. Families would arrive. The place
needed some sprucing up for long-range use.
We looked for ways to modernize the facility.

We had to face the reality that, although the
big house would accommodate our needs for
the time being, in six years or less the major
posts would begin rotting from constant exposure to rain. We also needed a better transportation system up and down the river if we
hoped to attract wives of missionaries or single

missionary women. (In fact, the first missionary woman to arrive complained about the difficulty she had navigating the hill from our
dock on the river up to the big house. I
laughed when I heard this. She should have
tried to climb that hill when it was nothing but
slippery mud, the way we found it.)

We tackled the problems in reverse order on
the theory that we needed a boat larger than a
canoe to handle the supplies we would need to
build a more substantial house. We discovered
a boat factory near Mazan on the Amazon
River. Friends of ours back in the United
States raised about $3,000 to purchase a mo-
torized launch twenty-five feet long with a
draft up to sixteen inches. It was powered with
a twenty-horsepower marine engine. The mail
boat towed it to our dock.

The new launch proved to be both a big help
and a big problem. As we hoped, we could
carry more supplies on it and when the water
level was high enough it moved faster than a
canoe. But the high water level was also the
rub. A three- to four-inch rainfall in one night
was not uncommon. When we were drenched
with one of these downpours, we had to spend
an hour or two bailing out the launch. On the
other hand, if the water level was low, the propeller could barely clear the rock reefs. Sometimes we got stuck on a bank with the propeller
spinning in sand creating a major maintenance
headache. Other times the propeller got tan-

gled up in vines or other growth we couldn't see under the river's surface. Occasionally we heard the sad sputtering of it dying because the blades hit a rock or a log. We began to anticipate problems and learned never to leave the big house without plenty of tools and patience.

The next task was to build a more substantial big house. With two years in Peru under our belts, we were now smarter about building materials. Since we had the luxury of more time to plan the project, we researched what was available in the jungle and what supplies we could order from the U.S. Then we mapped out a multi-staged program. We also divided up the responsibilities. The building would be sided with 12,000 linear feet of red cedar and roofed with galvanized iron. It would be equipped with glass windows rather than the open airholes in our walls which now passed for windows.

All this needed to be supported on a firm foundation. With my construction background, I was designated as the man for this job. I was proud to be chosen for this big responsibility— after all, I was the youngest man by nearly ten years—but I had no idea the amount of physical labor I had signed up for.

In my forays into deeper parts of the jungle I had discovered a type of tree that seemed ideal for blocks that would be reinforced underneath the new house by concrete footings. It was the ebony tree which, after it falls, sheds its outer layer of softer wood that rots on the moist jungle floor. This leaves a core of black wood so hard I couldn't cut it with an ordinary saw. I had to use a thirty-inch, fine-toothed handsaw over which I had maximum control to make even the slightest dent in this incredibly hard wood. The sawdust was like powder. The work was such slow going that I figured if I could cut just one block in the morning and another block in the afternoon, I would be doing well. I needed sixteen chunks that were each twenty-four inches long. I had to sharpen the saw eight times to cut those sixteen logs.

Each day I headed to the location where I had spied one of these fallen trees just ripe for cutting. So not only did I spend eight to ten hours each day sawing, I also had to travel by canoe to a spot considerably downriver from us, hike into the woods and then hike out again with my day's work.

One day, near the end of the project, when I was really looking forward to finishing and getting back home for supper, I stumbled and fell as I approached the canoe. The log rolled down the bank, plopped into the water and sank like a rock. I tried to retrieve it, but it was no use. The Pichis River claimed a perfectly cut ebony log twenty-four inches long. And I lost a half day's work.

Finally I had the sixteen posts in place plus the concrete footing. As a finishing touch on my foundation work, I dug a little canal around each post bottom and filled the trenches with water and kerosene. This would keep insects from crawling up the posts and into the house to be built above. Outwitting the pests became an avocation as well as a necessity during those years in Peru. At first they were just an annoyance. But later we learned the long-term health problems associated with insect bites.

Take fleas, for example. On the beach in Lima during our first year in Peru, we would watch fleas crawl out of the sand and up our legs. I later learned that I should have been constantly swatting them or shooing them away. I developed a high fever and was hospitalized for several days because of so many flea bites.

Another element we couldn't take for granted was sunlight. The ultraviolet rays penetrated the mist and fog in that part of the world which is below the equator. We learned the hard way what effect these menacing rays could have on skin. With all the rain in the jungle a sunny day was welcome. If we happened to be on the river when the sun was shining that was all the better. We might strip off our shirts and enjoy the warmth of the rays. Problem was, the sun was burning our skin. It was especially bad when direct sunlight was compounded with reflections off the water. Several times I was severely sunburned in just a short period of exposure. It took five or six years after I left Peru for my skin to clear up.

But it wasn't the natural elements that drove me out of Peru for a much-needed furlough at the three-year milestone of my tour. It was the vicious actions of evil men who wanted to kill me.

The following story is excerpted from an article entitled "Catholic Fury in Peru," written by Ray Clark, *The Alliance Weekly*, February 16, 1929.

At a few minutes before 8 o'clock on the night of December 1 we were hurrying through the back streets of Huánuco on our way to hold our third meeting in the fanatical section of the town known as San Pedro.

We had not been on the street long when we heard the church bells clanging noisily and in a way which would suggest the outbreak of a conflagration in the town. But it was not so. Rather it was the alarm to call the people together to break up the Protestant gathering.

We had previously been promised police protection, though this was only after prolonged effort before the authorities and against the determined opposition of the bishop and the clergy in general. By the providence of God we arrived at the house where we were to have our meeting before the storm broke—though only just in time. We had not been there more than a very few minutes when a hooting, yelling mob of infuri-

ated men, women and children bore down upon the house. We had the door open, but after the first volley of large stones hurled in at us we decided that caution was the better part of valor and closed the door.

By this time three policemen had arrived on the scene, who, on seeing the danger, sent for reinforcements. The mob was furious, and the stones were fast breaking in the door. Some of our group went to prayer while others guarded the doorway. We could hear outside such threats as: "Bring them out!" and "Kill them!" One woman screamed, "We will die here rather than give in!" Firecrackers were used to further excite the people and presumably to frighten us, while sticks and knives, we were afterward told, were apparent in the crowd.

During fully half an hour we remained thus trapped while the bells continued to call the people.

Suddenly the tide turned. Someone had just shouted, "We have orders to kill them!" when there was a sudden hush, an almost alarming silence, which was only to be broken a moment later by the quick shout of command by an army officer, "Attack them!" This was followed by a stampede. Twenty-five soldiers with drawn swords charged the mob of some 500 ill-humored, chagrined people.

As soon as the crowd had dispersed, we opened the doors of our little room and in-

formed the police that we would now start our meeting. In a very few moments the place was well filled with people, many of whom were perfect strangers to us, and a listening crowd gathered outside the door. I was happy to learn afterward that I had preached the gospel to the chief of police, the head of the military force and other officials.

13

The Real Enemy

S ometimes the enemies of the Lord come wrapped in the clothes of trusted people. Two examples come to mind. I'll begin with one that almost cost me my life.

We had been living off jungle food, not too tasty to our North American palates, but eventually we got used to it. What we missed most was anything made with good old-fashioned flour, such as biscuits. Finally, we ordered four fifty-pound bags of flour plus several cans of yeast and baking powder.

It had taken several seasons in the jungle for us to figure out the rhythm of the drastically changing weather. The idea was to place our order to arrive from New York during the rainiest time of year when the launches would be able to reach us. We made our plans carefully, mouths almost watering for the taste of those homemade biscuits, and finally sent for our shipment at just the right time. Or so we thought. For some reason, we had an early dry season, and the river went down which meant the launches couldn't make their deliveries. So our flour and the other supplies were stored in a warehouse in Iquitos until the rains started again and the river highway became deep enough to navigate.

We knew the flour probably would not be fit to eat by the time it arrived. Sure enough, it was molded. But something curious about one sack caught our eye. It had been opened and sewed shut by hand, whereas the other three flour sacks arrived just as they had left the mill in the United States. So we pulled out the string of that one sack, never imagining why it might have been opened.

Despite the foul smell of mold emitted from the bag, we decided to make just one little batch of biscuits. It had been so long since we had biscuits and, besides, the baking powder and yeast were fine.

Well, I baked the biscuits. They rose beautifully and looked yummy. Charlie and I each took a mouthful while they were still piping hot. Charlie immediately realized they were no good. He stepped over to the window and spit out his first bite. But I chewed mine a bit, enjoying the flaky texture while ignoring the foul taste. Rather than get up and spit it out, I swallowed that one little bite.

Although it was the only bite I actually consumed, it was a terrible mistake. Little by little I began to have trouble with my stomach. I thought it was just indigestion. And although the problem didn't completely incapacitate me, it grew worse over time. To flash forward a bit, let me tell you the horrible reality I eventually learned: in that one mouthful of biscuit I had swallowed enough ground glass to kill me!

It seems that the Jesuit fathers wanted us dead. As I learned throughout my years on the mission field, the "powers that be" can be quite corrupt when threatened by the shining light of the gospel. By encouraging people to know God, to learn His Word and to pray to Him directly, we were shaking up the status quo which had been keeping people in utter darkness. And shrouding the truth, of course, is one of Satan's favorite tricks.

Not long after my one bite of biscuit, I took my first furlough. I needed it, physically at least, because I had been battling malaria on and off, and now my stomach was giving me fits. For example, when I got back to the United States, I found that if I ate certain common foods—such as apples or pork chops—I immediately became severely ill.

I checked into Massachusetts General Hospital for diagnostic tests on my total digestive system. Cystoscopic machines had just been developed so that doctors could actually look into the interior of a patient's body—a modern marvel at the time. They used this machine to look down my throat and into my stomach. It was a big, awkward thing probably four or five times as big around as these tubes are nowadays, but I was able to swallow it anyway and let them take a look.

According to the doctor it was not a pretty sight. My stomach lining was like raw meat. The doctors tried to treat the problem, but they knew it was useless. In the meantime, they reviewed my complete medical history and, together with what we learned about how the Catholic Church was trying to drive out missionaries in South America, we pieced together what had happened.

All the evidence led back to the bag of flour that had been tampered with. Apparently it was a favorite trick to mix ground glass into such shipments bound for missionary camps. Leaving Peru for my furlough, I had questioned the customs authorities about their practices for handling food coming from the United States to missionaries. They had a good system for tracking invoice numbers at the dock and were able to determine exactly where that shipment had been stored and who had access to it before the goods were transported to the jungle. Of course, warehouse supervisors were not as forthcoming as the employees who finally admitted that when the Jesuit fathers came to the warehouse they were allowed to rummage among the shipments unattended because the priests were considered trustworthy. I imagine a few *pesos* across the palms of the men helped the *padres* gain entry. The more we asked around, the more we found that there had been other evidence of this kind of contamination and the two common denominators seemed to be missionary shipments and priests who wandered unguarded among the foodstuffs.

Fortunately for me and my stomach this story has a happy ending, but first I will relate another incident to illustrate the corruption we were in Peru to conquer with the help of the Lord.

Retracing our steps from the interior to the coast for my furlough, we stopped at some of the same villages we had seen during our first exploration trip. However, there was a big difference in our perception. After three years in the jungle, we were seeing the lives of these natives through our eyes which now were much wiser about the ways of pagan people.

On the way out we came upon a village of Amuexia Indians. We approached slowly, as we had the first time, until the natives recognized us as the men who had traveled before through their territory. We found the family that had provided us with hospitality by allowing us to sleep in a shed next to their house. After a bit of awkward communicating, I realized something was different. As the evening wore on, I tried to put my finger on what it was.

Finally, at some point I remembered. On my first visit to their home I had noticed a cute little boy about eight to ten years of age who was pretty rambunctious as I recalled. The youngster had the kind of behavior that would be considered slightly disobedient but still quite adorable in American families. It was the noise of his frisky teasing that was missing from this reunion. He was nowhere to be found.

"Didn't you have a little boy about so high?" I indicated with my hand held near my waist. I flopped my arms a bit to imitate the boy's erratic movements. They nodded and even told me his name. I asked what had happened to him.

"He's gone," they replied simply.

When I pressed for more, they shook their heads. No more information was available. After visiting with some other folks in the village, it became clear what had happened to the boy. Among these tribes the customary way to handle incorrigible children was rather severe to say the least. Because disobedience was considered a disgrace to the family—and, for that matter, to the whole tribe—a child like that would be killed and a conspiracy of silence among the tribesmen would cover the crime. And so this little boy had been taken alone into the jungle, murdered and buried there simply because he would not obey.

14

Prayer Warriors

I left Peru on furlough and arrived in Nyack just in time to give my testimony during the Friday night missionary meeting at the Missionary Training Institute. The camaraderie among the active and future missionaries was uplifting and encouraging. It was wonderful to be back.

With Christmas just a few days away, I traveled by train across the country to Phoenix to visit my family, a joyful reunion after three years. When they last had seen me, I was still a gangly teenager. Now, somewhat more mature, I had stories to share with family members eager for a vicarious trip to an exotic foreign land and with prayer warriors whose faith had saved me (literally!) from rough waters.

I will never forget one of those prayer warri-

ors. I had just related several anecdotes from
Peru at my parents' church when a lady in the
back raised her hand.

"Clyde," she asked, "did you keep a diary?" I
answered that yes, I had kept a diary and in-
quired why she wanted to know. She recounted
an amazing experience.

"One night I was awakened about midnight
and a voice seemed to say, 'Pray for Clyde Taylor. He's in great danger.' I immediately got
out of bed and prayed for about fifteen minutes. Then I felt the burden depart and so I figured you must be OK. I got back into bed and
went right to sleep."

After the service, as I rummaged through my
box of souvenirs and literature, I asked her if
she remembered the date. Just as I found my
diary, she came up with the exact month, day
and year from notes she carried in her purse. I
turned to that page and here's what I discovered: at precisely the same time in Peru, factor-
ing in the two-hour time difference, I was in a
life-threatening situation!

It started when we missionaries decided we
needed more banana plants. We arranged to buy
a canoe-load of plantain roots from some natives
near the headwaters of the river. The plan was
for me to pay the mail launch to tow our canoe
upriver and then I would return with the load
under my own power, just meandering downstream with the flow of the current.

On the appointed day I helped the Indian

merchants load about fifty of these large banana roots which weighed perhaps twenty
pounds apiece. Naturally, this weighed down
the canoe, and I recognized that it would be a
rough trip. I decided to stay the night.

About 1 o'clock in the morning I suddenly
awakened and noticed that the moon was full
and bright. It was almost as light as day outside
and I couldn't get back to sleep. I had already
paid for the plants, so I got up, dressed,
headed for the canoe and climbed in. It would
be a lot cooler to float downriver by the light of
the moon than to wait until daylight and endure the sweltering heat.

Quietly I pushed off from shore and pointed
the overloaded canoe into the swift current.
The scenery was breathtaking, and I was enjoying the solitude. With the bright moon I could
easily navigate around the huge rocks with my
paddle. *This is fortunate,* I told myself, *because
there are some mean rapids up ahead.*

I saw the foaming white water come into
view and got ready by grasping my paddle
firmly. The only way around the boulders
which created those rapids was a sure hand
and a clear eye. The huge rocks were just below
the water's surface and, at the speed the canoe
was traveling and with the weight I was haul-
ing, a miscalculated zig or zag could be disas-
trous. I knew that if we hit a rock the canoe
could break apart and I would land in the
water and perhaps be sucked under by the cur-

rent. *Fortunately, the moon is nice and bright,* I thought.

But just as I approached the rapids, a terrible thing happened! A thick cloud passed across the sky and obliterated the moonlight that only seconds earlier had illuminated the suddenly treacherous water. I couldn't see a thing. I braced myself for a crash, calling out to the Lord for protection.

Within a few moments it was over. The rapids were behind me and the sky had cleared. I looked over my shoulder at the churning water that I had traversed with absolutely no navigational help from me or my paddle. The canoe hadn't touched a single rock! It was such a spectacular moment of God's protection that I noted the incident in great detail in my diary when I got back to camp. And now in this church in Phoenix the Lord was connecting me with the very woman who had been awakened thousands of miles away to pray along with me. It was a powerful example of how God uses prayer to carry out His purposes.

My time in Phoenix was marred by the rages of malaria—attacks of chills and fever and occasional fainting spells. In addition, I was doubling up with stomach cramps due to the still undiagnosed effects of swallowing ground glass in the flour. So despite my mother's great cooking and the wonderful time I was having with my parents and brother, we decided I should return to the coldest climate possible, the only known treatment for malaria.

When the officials from headquarters offered to extend my furlough, I decided to spend the time studying at Gordon College in the cold climate of Massachusetts. And because my furlough was being extended for medical reasons, the Alliance agreed to continue my allowance during my education.

I was not altogether unhappy about living for awhile in New England. During the visit back to Nyack, when I was fresh from the mission field, I had met two sisters of my fellow missionary Charlie Marstaller. When he saw me off in Peru, Charlie told me to look them up. So on my first morning there I went to the dean of women and asked where I might find the two Marstaller girls. I learned that Esther was in class, but Ruth was helping out in the kitchen. I wandered in and found her peeling vegetables. Being a returning missionary, I was treated as sort of a privileged character, and so the staff was eager to point out to me the lovely young woman who had perched herself on a table because she was weary of standing up. That was the first time I ever laid eyes on my future bride.

I recall she had a rag wrapped around one finger because she had cut it while peeling. Being high-spirited and energetic, a little thing like a cut finger certainly didn't slow her down. And she had a great sense of humor. I could hear her laughing with the others in the kitchen. I liked that.

Later I asked permission from the dean of women to take Ruth and her sister downtown for an ice cream soda. This was a big request in those days. The institute was about a mile west of the town of Nyack. The girls walked into town on certain days and the boys on others. In other words, there were strict regulations about fraternizing, and so I wouldn't dream of going into town with Ruth, even with her sister accompanying us, without permission. Again, my special status as a missionary fresh from the field worked in my favor. I got permission.

Ruth and I wrote letters to each other while I was in Phoenix, and I hoped that I might be invited to the Marstaller family farm while I was at Gordon College. If Massachusetts wasn't cold enough to cure my malaria, surely Maine would be! Besides, I wanted to see more and more of Ruth.

From the first moment I laid eyes on Clyde, I recognized he was the type of man people looked up to—in more ways than one. Throughout our life together I continually told God how grateful I was and often asked Him, "Lord, how did You know to pick out

Clyde just for me?"

Ruth Marstaller Taylor
Durham, Maine

I soon got into the pace of studies at Gordon
College. But I was sick a lot and it became apparent that malaria wasn't the cause of most of
my discomfort. It was this constant problem
with my stomach. As noted earlier, I sought diagnostic help at Massachusetts General Hospital, which is where I learned that a foreign
substance—most likely ground glass which I
couldn't have tasted or felt with my teeth during the seconds the bite of biscuit was in my
mouth—had hit the lining of my stomach and
was wreaking havoc with my digestive system.

After the doctor and I concluded what must
have caused the problem, he prescribed some
remedies to help relieve the pain. What he
didn't tell me was that I probably had just a
few months to live. He saved that information
for the college president, Dr. Nathan Wood,
who had graciously taken a keen interest in me
as a student and a prospective leader (and, in
fact, I was elected president of my class every
year I was at Gordon).

Dr. Wood returned to the campus and, without my knowledge, gathered together the men
in the dorm. He told them the shape I was in
and what the truth was about how likely I was
to suffer a fatal hemorrhage. And then he got

their commitments to pray regularly for me, requesting that God heal my stomach. But he asked them to take care not to pray this particular prayer in my presence. The prayers continued for several months.

One day at lunch I eyed the pork chops. They seemed particularly lean, and besides, it suddenly dawned on me that I hadn't had much cramping or pain in my stomach for several weeks. So I speared a chop and tried a few bites. Nothing happened.

The next night they served apples after dinner, another food I had done without. Cautiously I reached for a big juicy one and sunk my teeth in with great relish. Again, nothing happened. No cramps, no pain, no indigestion, nothing.

In the following days I added other formerly forbidden foods to my diet. I never suffered another stomach pain, and there was absolutely no medical explanation for my healing. When it was finally concluded that the ordeal was over, I learned about the prayers of my fellow students.

Dad was the greatest prayer warrior of all. Even when at the end of his life his body was racked with the excruciating pain of cancer, he always got down on his knees and prayed.

Seeing him humble himself like that reminded me how, when I was a child getting up in the night for something like a drink of water, I would find my dad kneeling in the darkness, praying fervently. When I questioned him about it the next day, he would smile and say, "Oh, the Lord and I just needed to wrestle with a few things."

He taught me that God answers prayer. Later, referring back to some night when I'd found him on his knees, he would say, "I watched the Lord take care of that situation. When we do something His way, it always goes perfectly."

Orletta Taylor Gillikin
Arnold, Maryland

15

*Romancing
Ruth*

I set my sights on Ruth Marstaller. We spent
Christmas at her parents' farm in Maine.
For Valentine's Day I sent her a big heart-
shaped box of chocolates. I attended her
graduation from Nyack and drove her back
home. By now I felt confident enough to propose.

We had been offered the use of a charming—
and well chaperoned—cottage near Plymouth,
Massachusetts, owned by Dr. E.J. Evans, whom
we called Uncle Joe. He was general superinten-
dent of the Alliance in our area and also pastored a large Alliance church in Roxbury. Uncle
Joe had a keen interest in history and had saved
from destruction some artifacts related to the

Boston Tea Party. One was the fireplace in front of which the historic event had been plotted. When he learned the building was being torn down, he sent masons to break the fireplace apart into chunks, so it could be reassembled in his museum-like, antique-filled cottage. A housekeeper and groundskeeper lived there to maintain the house and its expansive grounds.

It was in that lovely setting that I proposed to Ruth on June 3, 1929. She accepted. We then went to Boston to buy an engagement ring and then on up to Maine for my next hurdle: gaining permission from Ruth's parents.

They had invited me to spend the summer with them rather than return to Phoenix where I would risk a return of the malaria symptoms because of the Southwest's heat. So I agreed to stay on the farm and help with the chores to pay for my room and board.

Mom and Dad were real romantics. Years later, while rummaging through a dresser drawer as a child, I discovered that Mom had kept that heart-shaped box Dad sent her when they were courting.

Carolyn Taylor Thompson
Oveido, Florida

Through the years Mom and Dad kept special tags they used for their Christmas gifts to each other. The tags were written in Spanish

*with loving sentiments meant only for the
other one's eyes. Their relationship was a
touching testimony of love between a husband
and a wife.*

Darlene Taylor Tate
Annapolis, Maryland

With so many family members present in the
rambling Marstaller farmhouse I found it almost impossible to catch Ruth's mother and father alone. In addition to Ruth's brothers and
sisters there were aunts and uncles, some of
whom also served as Alliance missionaries at
one time or another. It was a cheerful atmosphere full of hardworking, God-fearing people.

One summer day Ruth's father and I were
cleaning a chicken coop in one of the big hen
houses. I approached him by saying I had
something important to discuss. Whether he
knew the direction this conversation was heading I can't be sure, but he quickly persuaded
his wife to join us. I remember both of them
sitting on the edge of a roost while I talked to
them about marrying their daughter.

Mother Marstaller was a bit dubious about
whether Ruth was physically strong enough to
join me in my missionary work.

"Ruth was always one of the weaker children," she reminded me. I countered by pointing out that Ruth and I had prayed about this
and felt perfect peace of mind that our mar-

riage and work together was what the Lord wanted. We had turned our health over to the Lord. What's more, I told them Ruth had expressed to me her calling to work in Latin America. And I added that I couldn't marry anyone who wasn't called there as I knew I was.

That seemed to convince them.

"If you both are certain this is what the Lord wants, then we give our approval," Ruth's father told me. He added that they had no problem with me as their son-in-law.

I breathed a big sigh of relief and we went back to work.

The summer ended too quickly. I returned to Gordon College and learned that President Wood had arranged for me to become the chaplain at Thompson Island located in Boston harbor. A foundation operated a school on the island for boys who came from broken homes. The 130 students were taught trades such as printing, carpentry, plumbing and electrical work. My job was to catch a launch to the island on weekends and hold Sunday services.

Many of these students were deeply troubled. I witnessed to them about God's grace and tried to demonstrate that they were lovable despite their backgrounds. I also became involved with their basketball team which of course helped to win their confidence. I had the privilege of leading many of these boys to

Christ. Before the year was over, I put the figure of conversions at seventy-eight and saw significant changes in a great many lives.

Many of the new converts wanted me to baptize them. The problem, of course, was that I was not ordained. So President Wood made arrangements for my ordination at Tremont Temple in Boston, one of two churches where I had become active during my college years, the other one being Park Street Church, both near Boston Common.

Dr. Wood was a fantastic speaker. His ordination sermon was a masterpiece. We invited his father, a much loved, dear old saint who had been my professor of theology, to pray at the service. Ruth and several members of her family were present.

After my ordination I baptized the boys from Thompson Island using the baptistery at Ruggles Street Baptist Church.

It was several decades later when Clyde rushed into the street from his Washington, D.C. office at NAE and caught a cab for the airport. He noticed that the driver kept squinting at him through his rearview mirror and finally asked, "Your name wouldn't happen to be Taylor, would it?"

My husband replied, "Yes."

The driver said, "Clyde Taylor, is that right?"

Curious now, my husband leaned forward

*and noticed that the man had a text of
Scripture glued to his sun visor and a Bible
on the front seat. Clyde again replied, "Yes."*

The man's face broke into a broad smile.

*"You wouldn't recognize me, but I was one
of those boys you baptized from Thompson
Island."*

*He went on to tell how his life had continued
in service to the Lord with a good Christian
marriage, a day job and this moonlighting work
as a taxi driver. One story he told was how he
had led a passenger to Christ.*

*The man also shared with Clyde what he
knew about some of the other boys.*

*When they got to the end of the ride at the
airport, they prayed together. Later, Clyde
told me how gratifying it was to learn that
those troubled boys had remained faithful
and now led happy, productive adult lives.*

Ruth Marstaller Taylor
Durham, Maine

Ruth and I were married on June 7, 1930, at
the Marstaller farm. Dr. Joseph Evans offici-
ated at the ceremony. My best man was Merrill Tenney who was teaching at Gordon and
studying for his doctorate at Harvard. Merrill,
who later went on to teach at Wheaton College, was engaged to Helen Jadaquist, whose
father was in charge of publishing for The
Christian and Missionary Alliance office in

New York. I served as Merrill's best man a few months later.

We spent a month in Phoenix where Ruth met and got acquainted with my family. To escape the hot weather we spent the month of August at a cottage in California. We thought we would receive word any day of a missionary post opening up for us in South America. However, to our surprise we received a telegram from Dr. Wood inviting me back to Gordon for my senior year and guaranteeing me a student pastorate to pay our expenses. This was a delightful surprise because Gordon had a regulation against married students continuing in school without faculty permission. We headed back to Boston and settled into a tiny apartment. I enrolled in classes and pastored at First Free Baptist Church of Boston, located in Roxbury.

During my senior year, Ruth and I expected to hear from the Alliance. My hope was to return to Peru. But as I've said throughout my career, the Lord never sent me where I wanted to go. Yet He always knew best.

We were informed that the Alliance needed us in Colombia instead of Peru. So after another trip out west, we set sail on January 1, 1932.

Colombia was a country with soil and climate perfect for cultivating its greatest export in the early 1930s: coffee. We wondered if the political and spiritual climates were right for winning souls to Christ. We had no idea what hair-raising adventures awaited us.

Excerpted from "First Fruits in Colombia: Does It Really Pay?" by Rev. H.G. Crisman, *The Alliance Weekly*, June 5, 1926:

On Easter Sunday the Lord granted His workers now in Ipiales, Colombia, the first dividends on former investments by various workers. Nine precious souls buried with Christ in baptism; who can estimate their value?

They form the nucleus and charter members of our first [national] church. They have naturally become the target for much criticism and persecution in the town, and [I ask] your special prayers in their behalf.

Excerpted from "Intolerance in Colombia," by O.E. Langeloh, *The Alliance Weekly*, November 20, 1926:

Colombia is governed by the priests as no other country in South America. They govern marriage, and few there are that are not married by the church. The Roman Church insists that the marriage is valid only when it is performed according to the rites of the church and wherever she predominates she does not permit another kind. The strange part, however, is that only in Colombia has she been able to insist upon this point, because in all the other South American countries the States make the civil marriage obligatory.

The Roman Church purposes, at whatever cost, to possess the heart of the young by means of its colleges. Here they teach them with care the doctrines of their faith. If they can control the public instruction of the country, they consider it a supreme triumph, for it is then they can dominate both the people and the government. Very significant is it then that Colombia is the only Republic where public instruction is in her hands. The Roman Church desires to control the text, teachers and schools in all places as she does in Colombia, but she cannot.

What can be done? Colombia is virgin territory; many towns have never yet heard the glad story.

The people are prohibited from being friendly to us and the literature that we present to them is censored. It literally means excommunication for those who buy or receive it. The need of Colombia is Christ.

Excerpted from "Impressions of Colombia," by Rev. M.P. Zook, *The Alliance Weekly*, July 23, 1927:

Comparing Catholicism in Colombia with that of the United States or England, it would not be recognized as the same church.

There is no country in South America where the church is so securely entrenched as this one.

The Minister of the Government recently published a decree prohibiting the public propagation of the gospel in the country. If anyone appeals to the Constitution, which gives ample liberty for the preaching of the gospel, the authorities interpret the different clauses referring to this matter as they see fit, and it is useless to appeal to any higher authorities for they are all of the same mind and each supports the other. There is one very noticeable fact, however, and that is that the people themselves are very much more liberal than the authorities. The rank and file lament that religious liberty is so restricted.

Excerpted from "Missionary and Native Worker Jailed in Southern Colombia," by Oliver K.M. Cedar, *The Alliance Weekly*, April 6, 1929:

On entering San Dona we went to the home of a man who had bought a Bible some time before, and who was friendly toward the gospel.

After the service had continued sometime, we heard an awful racket outside the windows, which faced the street, and found it to be caused by a mob of people who were calling out, "Down with the Protestants." Then the alcalde [mayor] of the town with a num-

ber of other chief men entered the room, and
pronounced judgment against Señor Chingual and myself for doing public propaganda
in San Dona. Then he pronounced a verdict
of blasphemy against me, saying I had
preached [that] we believe in God but not in
Jesus Christ. So they told us the best thing for
us [was] to follow them to the jail, leaving our
possessions in the house of a friend.

When we got to the jail, the guards put
Señor Chingual and me in separate cells, so
we could have no communication. They
brought us each a mat to put on the floor, to
serve as a bed. The night before, at the home
of the man who was baptized, I had
preached about the Philippian jailer, and it
made us both laugh to think the experience of
being in jail was ours the next day.

About midnight the alcalde, with about a
dozen other men of the town, came to inform
us that the people had risen up against us,
[and they] were shooting off revolvers, and
that we had better leave San Dona at once.
They would get our horses ready.

Excerpted from "Intolerable Boldness," a
translation from a religious weekly published in
Popayan, Colombia, and published in *The Alliance Weekly*, June 22, 1929:

[Y]ou need warriors, and among the warriors there must be the civil authorities to guard

the Catholics against the bold and shameless Protestant propaganda, undertaken by the United States with the object, not so much to make Protestants, but to open an easier road to take possession of these coveted territories.

The followers of Luther, illegally called evangelicals, are working among us with a boldness that already passes the limit, and should preoccupy our government or . . . we will be absorbed by the United States. For patriotism we must open our eyes and declare war to the Protestant propaganda, not only for love of our holy religion, but also for love of our beloved country.

Excerpted from "The Power of the Gospel in Colombia," by Rev. W.H. Johnson, *The Alliance Weekly*, August 16, 1930:

The new President who assumes power during the present month, represents a more liberal wing than any administration of the last half century in Colombia. In a statement of official program, he expressed his intention to respect all religions tolerated in the republic. This is a new note, not heard during the conservative regime. Nor is it to be despised, for the gospel has only prospered on a large scale since the time of the Reform, in those countries whose princes (governments) have heard God more than the Pope.

Excerpted from "Difficulties of the Colombia Field," by Rev. W. Herbert Johnson, *The Alliance Weekly*, February 6, 1932, and printed with a photograph of Colombia's two newest missionaries, Rev. and Mrs. Clyde W. Taylor:

> *There is an intense hatred of the Bible on the part of the religious leaders of the country and a corresponding ignorance of the work of the Holy Spirit. The kind of literature most sought . . . [includes] lewd and coarse tales of illicit love.*
>
> *Satanic exorcism is practiced by some men in the cattle business, for the healing of sick animals. When a northern European asked a native whom he saw engaged in this form of sorcery if he did not fear consequences of such an awful practice he received the reply: "Oh, that's of no consequence. I'll confess next Sunday on market day, and the Padre will absolve me."*
>
> *Wife-beating is the usual approved method of bringing a more or less recalcitrant wife to see the error of her ways. The man who does not lie in a horse or cattle deal is the rarity if not a mythical being. In fact, I sincerely doubt the existence of any moral scruples, in connection with lying, on the part of the vast majority of Colombians. Liquor—native or Spanish wines—are essentials in every minor and major social function. A Colombian may even expose himself to the danger of be-*

*ing stabbed or shot should he persistently re-
fuse to accept a drink from the hand of an inebriated companion.*

*[T]hey are so weak in moral fiber that they
are generally cowed into trembling submission
by the religious leaders.*

*May the love of Christ, that passeth under-
standing, penetrate and bestow life eternal
upon the [Colombian] hearts.*

16

Armenia, Colombia— A Fighting Chance

R uth and I arrived by boat in Buenaventura, Colombia on January 19, 1932, and were met by Rev. Otto Langeloh, chairman of the Alliance field in Colombia. By the time we got through customs, the trains already had left for the interior, so we stayed in a hotel that night. The next morning we took the train to Cali, a distance of perhaps 120 miles that seemed much farther because of the ascent and descent over the western Cordillera mountains and into what was called the Cauca Valley. The Rio Cauca flows north from southern Colombia between the western and central ranges of the Andes.

We then traveled by train to the old Spanish city of Popayan, headquarters of the Alliance Mission in Colombia and home of the Langelohs. There we spent nine days with them enjoying a visit and trying to grasp the customs of the people.

The final leg of our journey was a quick stop in Cali to purchase a few household items and then the five-hour train ride into the Quindio Valley to Armenia. This would be our home for the next ten years. By establishing a Mission in Armenia we were not only reaching a new area for the Alliance, but also an area that had never had a missionary.

Armenia was not located in a developed area of Colombia. Most farms, buildings and houses were relatively new. Thirty years before our arrival the Colombian government had opened the area for homesteading much like the United States did to settle the West. Colombians could stake out a plot of land measured in hectares and this would become their property. Eventually, they would receive clear title to their land.

The triangular-shaped valley was hilly and ideal for growing coffee. Elsewhere in Colombia the hacienda system still existed with absentee landowners who lived in the capital city or in Europe and hired workers called "peons" to run their operations. In that feudal system, the landowners had absolute authority over whatever happened on their farms, including in the lives of the people who worked for them. Here in Armenia, however, the farms were individually owned.

When it came to evangelism, a typical scenario elsewhere in Colombia went like this: evangelicals would convert people living on the hacienda (farm), but then the local priest would find out and contact the bishop, who in turn would contact the owner. The next thing you knew your congregation would be removed overnight. But in Armenia, if a family accepted Christ, because they owned their farm, no one could dislodge them from their land.

In addition to the unique land ownership, many residents of the area around Armenia were blatantly anticlerical which created an atmosphere of some religious freedom. Of course the priests were not taking these attitudes sitting down. In fact, they felt very threatened and we were certainly most unwelcome by them and their avid followers. But we soon found out we had at least a fighting chance to convert the citizens who opposed them, that is, if we didn't get killed first.

We rented an apartment on the second floor of a house owned by one of the most radically anti-Catholic citizens. Just because he was opposed to the Church certainly was no guarantee that our landlord was open to the gospel. But it was a start.

We shared the house with the ex-mayor of

the city. All that separated our apartment from his was a partition that was only six feet high. That meant that a good four-and-a-half inches of my body were visible over the partition, which didn't give us much of a sense of privacy. But we eventually got used to it.

I had become pretty handy at woodworking, so I built most of our furniture including a head-board and an armoire for our clothes. We fash-ioned sofas out of army cots onto which we piled bedding. I even built our kitchen cabinets. Little by little, the place became livable as we assem-bled assorted items picked up at bargain prices.

Armenia was semi-modern but by no means on the cutting edge of technology. For exam-ple, water from all three of the city's hydroelec-tric power plants was plumbed into the house to ensure that at least one would be function-ing at all times.

Streets were paved with rocks, which became weapons in times of political fights and rallies. Roads outside the city limits were mostly mule trails. We had a terrible time finding any mules tall enough so that my feet didn't drag. We fi-nally settled on a horse—$25 for the horse and another $12 for a saddle. Often, however, I simply stuck out my thumb and caught a ride in a passing car when I needed to travel be-tween towns.

Eventually we came into contact with Er-nesto Viera. A committed Christian, this thirty-year-old man and his wife were friendly to us and willing to help us establish relationships. He had only the equivalent of a sixth grade education, but he knew the Bible well and he knew the local customs. Ernesto would be one of our keys to the city. By removing a wall in Ernesto's house we created a room that measured twenty-five by twelve feet, and so we began using that as our chapel.

Ernesto was good at distributing tracts. We arranged for a printing press to provide us with about 5,000 tracts per month. Handing out this many usually resulted in about one convert. It seemed like a lot of tracts to pass out but the ratio held steady, and so we continued with our order of 5,000 pieces of literature per month.

Slowly but surely we branched out and developed converts on outlying farms. Ruth and I realized that it would be productive to develop evangelists among the men who would have time after the coffee harvest to witness individually about Christ to their neighboring farmers. So by Christmas of 1932 two young men joined Ernesto and me in an intense Bible study. We began our sessions with a time of devotion and then studied whatever the two students felt they needed help in. Surprisingly, these young men had committed large blocks of the Bible to memory but had gaps in their knowledge about other things. For example, neither man had ever seen a map. They were fascinated with the maps printed in the back of our Bibles. So we spent many of our study sessions discussing how to use these maps to bring alive the stories of the Bible. They also knew very little about church history. Of course, when they discovered the abuses of the Catholic Church they were furious. Ernesto and I also spent a lot of time teaching them how to proclaim the gospel without simply denouncing the Roman Catholic Church. I believe you don't make converts to Christ by being "anti."

Our discipleship program grew. Between each coffee harvest we would accumulate a few more men. Eventually, by the end of four or five years, we had developed between 80 and 100 preaching points all over the valley and up into the mountains. Some of these groups consisted of as many as ten, twenty or thirty families. And, since the families in South America tend to be quite large, the congregations were good sized.

The natural result of all this was a lot of resistance from the traditional church. In fact, the local priest, Father Lopez, did us a real service by denouncing us so roundly and by preaching against us so vehemently. He warned the people not to listen to us, saying we were evil and dangerous. And so, human nature being what it is, a lot of his people, after hearing one of his sermons on Sunday morning, came to our little chapel on Sunday nights to see if all those heresies were true.

With all the negative publicity given to us by the Roman Catholic Church, plus the distribution of literature, the daily visiting around the city and the weekly forays into the countryside, we began to grow. But we really grew by leaps and bounds when Father Lopez changed his tactics from verbal to physical threats, even against my life. By being such a fanatic, he encouraged people to take sides. When a man's life is at stake, people tend to jump onto one bandwagon or another.

Lesson one: The more you persecute the Church, the faster it grows.

17

A Price on My Head

We discovered that the Colombian priests of that era were real fire-eaters. There were explanations for this, given the history. For one thing, they were all Iberian—that is, from European countries such as Spain and Portugal. They therefore believed in an inquisition and virtually declared war on Protestants. They would do anything to stomp us out, no matter how brutal the intimidation—or worse—the killings. Anything was considered fair game to get rid of the evangelicals.

Father Lopez eventually honored me by putting a price on my head. He put the word out among his followers that he would pay the princely sum of $300 to anyone who would murder me. He added several other incentives to sweeten the deal. Not only would he give them

$300, but he would also protect them from the law. Whoever carried out this crime would be exempt from legal punishment. What's more, they would go straight to paradise, skipping purgatory altogether, spending eternity in heaven. The events of the next few years made it obvious that many considered this a pretty good deal.

The 1930s and '40s were ugly years in the history of the Roman Catholic Church. For centuries South America had been a Catholic stronghold. During the early part of the twentieth century and until the more enlightened and reasonable Pope John the Twenty-third ascended to power, resistance was almost overwhelming to any religious belief which emphasized a personal relationship with Jesus Christ. Ironically, the priests should have known that people who make a personal acquaintance with the Lord continue to need a certain hierarchy of God-ordained leaders to shepherd them throughout their lives. But the priests and bishops nevertheless were threatened, probably because if their flocks knew the truth it would illuminate their wicked ways.

Almost as soon as we arrived we learned of instance after instance of the local Catholic *padres* fathering illegitimate children or stealing from the very people who looked to them for moral guidance. And so it was understandable that they feared a change in their corrupt control over the citizenry. Of course, God was big enough to overcome such resistance, but He allowed me to be tested by direct threats on my life. And He used those circumstances to show the people the clear distinction between good and evil.

We, as children and adults, knew above all that Dad's core dependence was on the Lord. His reputation as a large yet humble person was lived out in our family.

I suspect that, like other missionaries of his day, he was challenged by the human face of our evangelical community and—to speak candidly—by the carnality and sin in the lives of some men who professed Christ. I'm sure these problems wore Dad down at times and certainly frustrated the pursuit of those objectives of Christian unity in ministry that he believed God had given him. But what our family saw repeatedly was that these problems also drove him to prayer and to a tighter dependence on our Lord.

Dad's faith was not pie in the sky but a Christian walk in which it was obvious that God was achieving in him a strong integration of faith and practice.

Clyde Donald Taylor
Washington, D.C.

Father Lopez made his plans very public. Many friends of the evangelical movement in

Armenia would go to his Sunday services and come to our little chapel in the evening to report what scheme he was hatching. They were sincerely afraid for my life. I didn't take the problem too seriously at first—but then I began having some very narrow escapes.

For example, one morning Ruth and I spent a long breakfast deciding that the time had come for me to begin discipling lay evangelists in the outlying areas. We spent our morning meditation time reading Scriptures to confirm our sense that this was where our ministry was leading, and then we prayed about it. It was a deliberate plan that we discussed for the first time that morning, and, of course, we had not shared it with anyone.

After breakfast I caught one of the cars that was heading in the direction of Helvecia. The driver dropped me off about two miles from my destination, and I walked the rest of the way. To my utter amazement, when I got there and found the principal evangelical, he told me that he had already been informed by the priest that morning that I was on my way and what would be the purpose of my visit. This was a real puzzle because I myself had not known until about 8 o'clock what I was going to do! The only conclusion I could make was that Satan had informed the priest. God certainly hadn't. It demonstrated how active and real were the forces of evil and how Satan would try to interject himself into efforts that he wanted to thwart.

Of course, the priest knew exactly what he was doing. By suggesting that he could read my mind, he was beginning a psychological warfare that soon would take on more serious dimensions.

The *padre* left a message for me to stay in Helvecia after I had conducted my business. I made it clear that he did not set my schedule, and so, after discussing the discipling idea with several prospective converts, I told the rather anxious bystanders that I had no desire for an argument with the priest. I left, setting out on foot in the direction I had just come a few hours earlier. Suddenly I got a strong inclination to cut across a coffee field about one mile square.

Coffee plants grow fifteen to eighteen feet high, but the workers cut them off at about six feet. This meant I could see over the tops and tell where I was headed, although the average Colombian was at least six inches shorter. I began to zigzag through this field in a diagonal direction.

After a few minutes of walking I heard hoofbeats thundering down the trail bordering the coffee field. I realized it was the priest accompanied by many riders. I crouched below the level of the plants and made my way to the road on the other side. Fortunately, I was able to quickly hail a passing car.

Later I learned that Father Lopez had returned with coffee pickers (extremely strong men to begin with!) who were armed with machetes—enormous, heavy knives used for whacking thick underbrush. Of course, they also make excellent—and deadly—weapons. The plan was for the priest to get into a discussion with me and elevate it to a hot argument. Then he would call in these people to liquidate me. It would have been a bloody death with no witnesses to tell whether I truly had threatened him so that he had justification to call in his armed musclemen. I figure the Lord got me out of that situation with between five and eight minutes to spare.

Another time a man came to our house and pretended to be genuinely interested in the gospel. He then invited me to come down to *la tienda,* the store and bar that served as a local meeting place for speeches. He said that he had some friends he wanted to assemble to hear my message. I agreed enthusiastically, and so we set up a date and time.

Minutes before I was on my way out the door to attend the meeting, one of the Christians in the area came rushing into our house. He was sweating from running to get word to me that this event was a setup. Seems he had overheard two *braggadocios* in a bar. A couple of drunks with loose tongues were discussing the plot to show up with machetes and guns. Again, the plan was to draw me into an argument, claim I had become a threat to the priest and then kill me to "protect" the good *padre.*

After about two years of such incidents, the weapons of choice switched from knives and guns to stones.

A group called the *Maristas* or Sons of Mary ran a school for 500 boys on the mountainside just outside the city limits. (Several years later, this became the site of our Bible school.) The students were elementary age through what we would call junior high school. Every afternoon on their way home they would detour past our house and throw stones against our wall. It made a tremendous noise and was very disruptive. It became such a regular event that I could almost set my clock by it. Keep in mind that these were not just youngsters out having a raucous good time at my family's expense. They were incited to do this as intimidation by the Catholic powers that be.

Every now and then, a rock would come over the top of the roof and land in our patio. One day when our daughter Orletta was about five months old and lying in her buggy, a rock the size of a man's fist came sailing through the French doors and missed the baby by just a few inches.

"That's it!" I said to Ruth as I headed out the door after the boys. I had no intention of running after them, but I knew I could overtake them on my bike. On that day there were three boys. As soon as they saw me swing open the door and jump on my bike, they headed off in three directions. I took off after one who turned into a side street which I knew to be a dead end but he apparently didn't. So I pedaled after him until he was cornered. He had to face me. The kid was so frightened that he wet his pants. But I didn't touch him. I asked him what his name was and where he lived. Trembling, he told me.

"OK, let's go to your house and see what your father has to say about this," I said in a firm voice. He walked along beside me, obviously shook up about what might happen next.

We arrived at his house as his father was dismounting from his horse. He had just ridden in from their farm out in the country. Father and son exchanged glances, and I wondered if the man would support the boy's behavior or discipline him. I was hoping for the latter.

I told him what had happened and explained that this had been going on for weeks. The father turned to his son and asked if what I was saying was true. The boy admitted that it was. The man was furious. Seems he was not so much of a fanatical Catholic that he wanted an American to get stoned and thus risk getting his family into trouble with the police even though I had not threatened to bring them into the matter. Immediately he removed one of the big straps from his horse's saddle and steered his son to the back of his house. Before I was on my way, I could hear the sounds of a thrashing.

It stopped the stoning, but that's not quite the end of the story. As usual, God found a way to use even that incident for good.

A few weeks later I passed a large group of these schoolboys on the street. I recognized three of them from the day of the chase and others in the group from earlier stonings. They were surprised when I spoke up as we were about to pass.

"You are some of the fellows who were stoning our house," I said. They looked startled that I would speak to them, but I continued. "All you did was hit the wall or pitch a rock into our patio, but if you were trained in baseball you would have better pitching arms." And with that, I reached down for a large stone in the road and gripped it like a baseball pitcher. Immediately, they began to scatter. I shouted, "No, wait. Watch. I'll show you how to pitch." I heaved the rock at a telephone pole about fifty feet away and hit it dead-on. Then I picked up another, wound up like a pitcher and again hit the post. I did this over and over again while they stood spellbound with childlike wonder.

Finally one boy asked how I could do that with such good aim and I told them that I used to pitch on a baseball team. Boys being boys, suddenly I was their hero! They asked if I would teach them baseball. Unfortunately, I said, "No, I'm afraid I don't have time because of all my responsibilities as a missionary."

Later I regretted turning them down when I realized what a tremendous investment of my time that would have been, bringing the sport of baseball to this town, organizing teams and winning the confidence of people in still another way. But no, I didn't have sense enough to do that. We had never been taught that teaching sports to kids could be one step toward winning their parents for Christ. But I did accomplish something that day—I helped these boys realize that Protestant missionaries were real people they could relate to.

Dad was always in a hurry to expose every soul in town to the gospel. Although he was a wonderful family man, he knew what a tremendous responsibility he had to the native Colombians.

I remember once when a man was gored to death by a steer that got loose in the market. A few months earlier Dad had presented the gospel to him, but he had rejected it. We watched sadly as men carried his casket up the hill to the cemetery. His widow and children followed behind, wailing loudly along with the grieving townspeople.

"Only the Lord knows if there's any hope for that man's resurrection," Dad lamented. "But I keep thinking I should have done more."

Orletta Taylor Gillikin
Arnold, Maryland

18

Father Lopez
Ups the Ante

Our enemies were not above picking on children. The people who wanted us silenced even tried to frighten our children.

We had been in Armenia for a few years when two-year-old Orletta ran into the house crying. She had been playing with her favorite ball on the front doorstep next to the sidewalk when some boys came along. They snatched the ball away from her, slapped her hard on both cheeks and called her names. Then they calmly walked away, taking the ball with them.

Again, about a year later, Orletta came screaming into the house and holding her hand over one ear. This time she had been playing with her doll. A man had come by, pulled her long curls and then stuck the lit end of his cigar into her ear, all the while calling her "a d——

Protestant." When Ruth got the full story out of Orletta and pulled her hand away from the ear, the ashes were still burning. She quickly cleaned them out and dabbed oil to ease the pain. Then she went downstairs with Orletta and found the man still standing on a nearby corner, bragging about his great accomplishment.

By the time I came home from a Bible class, the man had left. In a sense, I thank the Lord for this timing, because I was so upset when I found out what he had done, I might have rushed to the corner and faced an armed man just itching to kill me. Thankfully it didn't happen.

There were many other such incidents which were precursors to the growing unrest in Colombia. The ultimate result was a sort of guerrilla warfare between the liberals and the conservatives in which the Roman Catholic Church became active in trying to liquidate the liberals. Even in the twentieth century, religious fanatics can be brutal in any part of the world. Many Protestants were caught in these battles. Chapels were burned, pastors were killed and whole congregations fled for their lives. It became know as *la violencia*, the violence.* Most of this

---

* The Alliance lost nearly sixty chapels, dynamited or destroyed by fire. According to *Historia del Cristianismo Evangelico en Colombia*, by Rev. Francisco Ordonez, "Twenty-seven percent of evangelical churches were reduced to ashes. One-hundred-and-ten primary schools were closed by official order or due to armed violence."

took place after we left the country, but we were witnesses to what led up to it and, of course, had many close calls ourselves.

One incident that happened at Barcelona demonstrated just how far the influence of Father Lopez stretched.

Ruth and I were invited by a small group of Christians to hold a meeting in the home of a widow named Señora Maria. The converts thought maybe we could attract some of their neighbors. So we persuaded a dozen Christians from Armenia to go with us and rented a bus for the twelve-mile ride.

When we arrived, we set up a small folding organ and began to sing hymns. Within minutes, the bells of the church down the street began ringing violently, normally the alarm for fire. We looked outside. In no time fifty to seventy-five people had formed an angry mob.

The town's only policeman also arrived armed with an old-fashioned .45 revolver in a hip holster. Although he was the only policeman in town, he was dressed in his formal uniform. He had a whistle that he was using rather liberally despite the continual clanging of the church bells. Positioning himself between the crowd and the door, he requested that we stop playing the instrument and singing. He informed us in a very matter-of-fact manner that it was "irritating" to the townspeople.

That seemed like a fair request, so I agreed to it. Throughout the rest of our toned-down service he stood in front of the house with one hand on the "cannon" in his holster as if daring the crowd—which had not dispersed—to come any closer.

We finished the service and packed up the organ. I stepped outside and told the officer that we had a bus parked around the corner. He indicated that we could leave the house to board the bus. The still attentive crowd followed us there en masse and the policeman momentarily fell behind. Just as we were climbing into the bus, the crowd went out of control. They picked up rocks and began lobbing them, breaking the windshield and denting the sides of the vehicle. The policeman finally broke up the riot by shooting his gun into the air.

Later we learned that the crowd had been organized by Father Lopez.

By now we had groups of Christians throughout the valley, and every now and then one of them would be attacked. A believer named Ramon had a very humiliating experience in his little town of Tabaya.

Just a few days before I was scheduled to speak there, the local priest, along with an accompanying crowd, paid a visit to Ramon. He began threatening Ramon because he had been preaching about religious faith, although, as the good father pointed out at the top of his lungs, Ramon was not a Roman Catholic priest. The people seemed to enjoy watching the poor man endure the lecture. Suddenly, the priest stepped closer and slugged Ramon in the face, so hard that his eye swelled and later became black-and-blue. But Ramon stood his ground and calmly pointed out what the Bible says: if your enemy hits you on the face, turn your other cheek. He asked the priest if he would like to hit him on the other side of his face. Unfortunately, the priest complied.

A murmur spread through the crowd and many began shaking their heads. The priest had lost the people's respect. Had Ramon not behaved more like a Christian than the priest had? They had seen God's love and truth in action.

I'm so grateful that the enemy never seemed to learn that valuable lesson: The more you persecute the Church, the faster it grows. When I arrived a few days later, the crowd that assembled for our service was bigger than ever. However, the building had once been a store with a large window that fronted on the main street. From where I stood I could see the priest assembling a crowd soon after the service began.

Just as I began my sermon, to my utter amazement a stick of dynamite came flying into the building. It landed just in front of the pulpit. Someone had put about an eighteen-inch fuse on it, then lit it and threw it into the building at the most dramatic moment. Naturally, the worshipers recoiled in horror. Some buried their heads in their arms or scurried to the sides of the room, which wouldn't have done much good if it had gone off. But because of my days in the construction business in Phoenix, I had seen a lot of dynamite and knew that time was on my side with a fuse that long. I calmly stepped to the front of the pulpit, picked up the stick and threw it back out into the street. The crowd out there parted like the Red Sea and our own people huddled together inside as far away from the window as possible. The dynamite blasted a hole in the street about two feet deep.

This was the only time they tried to dynamite our services, although when the political wars broke out some years later dynamite was often used to start the fires that burned down our chapels.

One Sunday morning I caught the 7 o'clock train and rode through a series of towns to hold a meeting in Montezuma. The railroad station was about four blocks from the house where the local evangelist lived and where we were going to hold both a worship service and a Sunday school class. The new converts needed to be educated and by combining teaching with worship I could help the evangelists who were trying very diligently to keep their flocks together.

Sunday was also market day in Montezuma, and soon we had attracted our usual hostile crowd peering into the house. Halfway through, there were at least 200 people gathered outside the French doors trying to get a look at us. I tried to ignore them but all of a sudden one rough-looking man who identified himself as a butcher stepped forward with a twenty-two-inch knife. A hush fell over the service as everyone turned around and strained to look.

"I have come to cut your throat," he announced. I decided that was a good time to pray, and so we did. While we had our heads bowed, two local policemen showed up. Neither they nor the man with the enormous knife stepped inside the room—they remained at the open door. One officer demanded that we stop singing "because it bothers the people in my town." I nodded that we would not sing and switched to the lesson.

The man with the knife continued to glare and the police did nothing to move him away from the doorway. I found it a little difficult to concentrate on a Sunday school lesson with a man ready to cut me up. When I finished most of what I had come to say, I gathered up my Bible, my briefcase and my hat and started for the door.

The people in the congregation were aghast.

"Where are you going?" they asked.

"It's time for me to catch my train," I replied. They tried to talk me out of it by saying I could catch the next one after the crowd outside had dispersed and the butcher got tired of waiting. But I felt strongly that I had to put my foot down on this intimidation and so I stepped to the door and said as politely and nonthreateningly as possible, "*Con sus permisos, señores,* (With your permission [excuse me], gentlemen)."

By now the mob was so large that when they opened a four-foot pathway for me to walk through, the crowd on either side was about twelve feet deep. I turned my back to the man with the knife that was nearly two feet long and no doubt freshly sharpened and continued walking the four blocks to the railroad station. Many in the crowd kept pace with me, wondering if the butcher would suddenly spring and start a bloody attack.

What I remember most about that four-block walk was how utterly calm and peaceful I felt. I recognized that calmness to be coming directly from God. It was probably my saving grace. If I had given the man any indication that I wanted a confrontation, I'm sure he would have obliged by killing me on the spot even though the police were watching.

Voices behind me were saying, "Don't you see that the Protestant is getting away?" But I just continued walking, feeling more at peace with each step. I think that in those few minutes I captured a sense of what the martyrs may have experienced, the pure grace of God and the assurance that He is with you every step of the way.

A week later, when the priests brought a mob to attack that same chapel, the military was waiting. They confiscated machetes and guns from the unruly crowd and arrested a few of the more vocal men. They also ordered the priests to leave. And that ended that.

19

The Missionary
versus the Monsignor

I was more than ready for a breakthrough
with the Catholic hierarchy when the Lord
graciously provided one.

Our Armenia congregation had grown to the
point where we were renting and filling a hall
that fronted on the main street through town.
The location was well-known throughout Armenia, one factor in the success of attracting
potential converts. We drew fifty to seventy-
five people each service.

One Sunday evening as we were about to
start the service, we heard a crowd assembling
outside. The people were focused on a man positioned across the street. He would shout
something, they would let out a cheer and then
they would turn to look in my direction. It was
obvious he was trying to draw a reaction out of
me, and they were looking forward to it.

As I stepped to the window I saw that the man was peering down at me from the second story of the building across the street. Immediately I recognized that his words would carry better than mine. Also, because he was positioned above me, he had a symbolic advantage. I drew a deep breath, prayed a quick but silent prayer and got ready.

It became clear who he was—the monsignor from Manizales, which was the capital of the province. I found out later that he had made the trip to Armenia especially to have this debate with me.

The man was quite an orator. He would bellow out his accusation with a flair for the dramatic, pause at just the right moments and then, as if on cue, the crowd gathered in the street between us would cheer their admiration and support for him.

He accused me of using a phony Bible. He called it a Protestant Bible by which he meant it was different than his and therefore false. With that, I reached for our Spanish translation and offered it up to him.

"I beg your pardon, sir. Would you like to examine this? It's the Roman Catholic Bible translated by your own Father Amat. This is what we're using."

He appeared flustered. To cover his embarrassment the crowd filled the silence with angry shouting directed at me. But the most curious part of their choreographed performance was that, whenever I would speak, the children would begin chattering to cover up whatever I was saying. The monsignor held the most remarkable hold over a crowd I ever saw. Even the little ones were cooperating with his efforts to win the debate!

More people began to gather, including some of the town's most influential businessmen. Word had gotten around that a riot was going on down at the Protestant chapel. Before long, people began picking up rocks from the street in preparation for the fight.

A policeman stepped into our chapel.

"Mr. Taylor, would you mind stopping this discussion?" I informed him that I didn't start the discussion. I pointed my finger out the window, motioned toward the monsignor on the second story balcony across the street and said, "He came to town to challenge me, and he brought the crowd to this street with him." I added that I wasn't accomplishing much anyway because the monsignor had the children trained to make a racket whenever I opened my mouth.

The officer crossed the street, went into the building and appeared a few moments later on the balcony. The crowd hushed. The monsignor announced with a loud voice that he was willing to discontinue because "I've won the argument anyway." With that comment the crowd broke into a loud cheer. The monsignor directed everyone to meet him at the Catholic church a few blocks away where they were going to shoot off fireworks in celebration of their victory over the Protestants.

As the crowd began to disperse, I sat down for a few moments to rest. The tension of the debate and the stress of the shouting had exhausted me. Suddenly I looked up and found several of the town's most prominent businessmen coming into the chapel. These were store owners and farmers with the largest coffee plantations. I stood up and shook hands all around. They thanked me for what I had done. Somehow they had managed to hear me above the noise and realized I had won the debate, although it was the monsignor who was celebrating. But more importantly, these men wanted to hear more.

Even though I was hoarse by then, I invited them to sit down and I stepped up to the pulpit. I proceeded to explain, not in sermon-style but just man-to-man like a conversation, why Jesus had come to earth and died for our sins. I talked about God's grace and His plan of salvation. I explained what it took to become a Christian. I told them about eternal life.

Several said they were interested in learning more and promised to come back for a service. (And they made good on that promise, I'm happy to add.) After my explanation was over, each man shook my hand warmly and thanked me for sharing what I think they all sensed was the most important information they could ever hear.

Besides the salvation of many of those men, credibility for our missionary effort was established in the eyes of the leaders who would be key to our success in establishing the Armenia Bible Institute. After that day, whenever I needed supplies such as lumber I approached these men and they generously donated money or goods. When I went into their places of business, including the main store in town, the Buen Gusto, I handed out New Testaments with their full approval. So by bringing these businessmen to this particular meeting and by opening their hearts to the gospel, the Lord's timing was perfect. We were growing rapidly, and we were developing needs that required the support of these men.

When converts wanted to be baptized we constructed a wooden tank about six feet wide by eight feet long and three feet high. It took a lot of labor and materials to build because it had to be water tight. Some people wanted to be baptized in running water, like Jesus. We fulfilled those requests in the Rio Quindio.

But the most lasting contribution these men made was to the building of our Bible Institute, the effort that was our real legacy in Colombia.

20

The Most Unlikely People

Just as in Jesus' day, the Lord drew people to Him that many of us would dismiss. One of our first converts was Don Felix. He became such an effective witness that we trained him in the Bible classes that were to become the forerunners of our Bible Institute. But Don Felix ("Don" may be translated "Mr.") had an unlikely background for an evangelist. He was an ex-murderer who had been thrown into prison for killing a man!

As the story goes, he was in a big card game. They were poor people so they weren't gambling for high stakes, at least as far as money was concerned. But when you add whiskey to the mix, then anything is bound to happen.

Don Felix got into an argument with a fellow player and wound up killing him over a *peso*. That kind of brutality was not uncommon, and the prisons were filled with men such as him. In fact, the prisons were overflowing and so, after about eight years of his sentence, Don Felix was let out for no other reason than that they needed his cell space.

As an ex-convict he still had a feisty attitude. So one day when he heard from a priest at mass that someone was selling "an awful book that no one should read" Don Felix was ornery enough to begin seeking that book. The book of course was the Bible. Although he was barely literate, he spent time working his way through it and believing what it said. Eventually he sought out one of our evangelists, made a public confession of faith and became a fearless witness to working-class men.

So Don Felix joined our small group in Bible study, learning Scripture, studying doctrine, church history and, like the other students who had never traveled more than a few miles from home, poring over maps. I could never get over how fascinated those people were with maps! Those of us who have had the blessing of travel can hardly relate to the thrill of seeing for the first time an illustration on paper of how the world is laid out.

Another convert was named Don Angel. He owned a successful coffee plantation but over the years he had become a hopeless drunk. He was known to be cruel and brutal as well as often armed and dangerous. His whole family had been affected by his alcoholism. But he overheard some people talking about the gospel and invited us to his house to explain it. Somehow, through the maze of his drunken stupor, he understood the message and made a decision to follow Christ. It was an immediate transformation. He never again touched another drop of liquor.

Don Angel brought us back to talk to his whole family who by now were ecstatic about his life change, which he described as "from hell to heaven." He became such a bold witness for the Lord that whenever we went into his part of the valley he offered his home for the meetings and drew a large, enthusiastic group.

A man named Ruben Torres lived across the Quindio River from Armenia. He too traveled to our meeting place and turned to Christ. His house also became a place of worship, one of the many house churches that sprang up.

A couple of years later he rented out his coffee farm and moved into town. Unknown to him, the house he moved into was right next door to a brothel owned by a very obese prostitute who by then was about forty-five years old and the mother of a house full of illegitimate children.

Ruben had the custom of sitting in his doorway and reading his Bible aloud. Many of our converts did this. They seemed to think they could live it better if they not only understood it with their hearts but heard it with their ears.

One evening about dusk he was reading aloud when, about six feet away, the prostitute and two of her daughters (who had joined her in the profession) sat on their doorstep and began to listen. Occasionally, when he would pause and read silently for a verse or two, she would call out and ask him to speak up. She was following every word.

They sat outdoors all night long, the light from his doorway illuminating the pages. By dawn they had finished at least three of the Gospels. At the end he challenged the prostitute and her daughters to accept Christ as their Savior, which they did. They became such effective witnesses that from those two households grew one of the largest and most faithful congregations in the area.

Ultimately, the oldest son of Don Ruben attended the Bible Institute, graduated and became one of our best workers.

Baptisms in and around Armenia could be very humorous. Some converts wanted to be baptized in our three-foot deep outdoor baptismal tank. Occasionally we would get a very rotund convert. On those occasions I would gently lower the new believer under the water but, in order for it to be official, all of the body needed to be immersed. So sometimes I would have to press down on the convert's stomach. This always brought a roar of laughter from the crowd.

The first time we had a group baptism in the river the police came running down the slope to the edge of the bank shouting at us to stop. Apparently word had been delivered to the police department that the Protestants were down at the river drowning people. When the truth came out, this brought a big laugh. So our baptisms were always thought of as happy occasions.

I quickly learned that a missionary has to be flexible.

One day Don Ernesto and I were visiting a family that had accepted Christ. They had opened up their home the night before and we enjoyed a meeting with about ten other families. The next morning Don Ernesto approached me from the kitchen. The hostess was going to serve tripe (cow's stomach) for breakfast, but Don Ernesto came to warn us that she had not cleaned it properly for missionary consumption. It would cook nicely and look tasty but he knew from experience that the tripe would cause us to vomit.

I asked him how long after the meal that would happen. He estimated about fifteen minutes. So we devised a plan. I suggested that we have devotions with the family and get our horses packed and ready to go before sitting down to breakfast.

"Right after we eat, Don Ernesto and I will have to leave," I explained to the hostess.

And so, almost as soon as our last bite of breakfast was eaten, we gave them a big smile and started on our way. We just managed to get out of town before we had to leap off our horses and leave our breakfast by the side of the road.

A story one of my workers told was even worse.

Jorge had been visiting in a home when the lady of the house announced, "Lord willing, to-morrow we will have meat for breakfast."

Jorge was sleeping in the attic which he accessed by climbing up a notched pole. During the night Jorge heard his hostess come up the pole and set out something which he recognized to be a trap. *Oh, no,* he lay there thinking to himself.

The next morning she indeed served a breakfast of meat. She had caught and roasted a big fat rat!

Jorge told this story to the students at the Bible Institute. They were amazed that he would eat it. But Jorge told them, "I didn't want to risk the Lord's work by not accepting her hospitality. She thought this meal was generous.

On the mission field you eat what's set before you. You don't say you don't like it."

Missionaries working in a Catholic country soon learned that many couples, even those who have professed Jesus Christ as their Savior, often never bother to get married. That's especially true of the poorer ones, because the biggest expense for a wedding is paying the priest to perform the service. So many never get around to it. They were considered common law husband and wife, and by our standards their children were considered illegitimate. As we gained their confidence we would confront them with the rightness or wrongness of not participating in this ceremony and making their relationships official in the eyes of the Lord.

Because all marriages had to be performed by the Catholic church to be legal, Protestant missionaries did not conduct weddings. But we encouraged and discipled our followers to do this and often attended ourselves. It was not unusual to have a double ceremony with a mother and father getting married first, followed by one of their children and the parents' new son- or daughter-in-law. And, to top it off, the double wedding might be followed by the christening of grandchildren!

Buen Gusto was the store in town where we got most of our supplies for the Bible Institute. The owner and top managers had been among the men who came to our chapel after my public debate with the monsignor. Over the years they became some of our biggest supporters. Here I will flash forward a bit.

In the 1960s, when I was traveling around the world on behalf of WEF and other organizations, Ruth and I were back in Colombia. We were staying in Cali, one of the largest cities. In the intervening years many people from small towns such as Armenia had abandoned their businesses and fled to the cities to escape the persecution that often accompanied their conversions.

One day I was called to the phone and heard a vaguely familiar voice at the other end. The man reminded me who he was—an assistant manager of the Buen Gusto store in Armenia nearly thirty years earlier. He told me a fascinating story.

While he was happy to see me whenever I came into the store, he admitted that he really never read the New Testament I had given him until many years later. After he and his family fled to Cali, when they unpacked their trunks at their new home, he was feeling particularly discouraged and despondent because the move had cost him his entire life savings. It would not be easy to start over financially at that stage in his life. So he was taking his time about going through the items in the trunks, mulling over everything.

Finally he pulled out the New Testament,

dusted it off, carried it into his bedroom and began reading it. His reading continued for several more days until he finished the whole volume. Although he had taken a stand for Christ and against the brutal regime of the Roman Catholic Church, he had never before those long days of reading Scripture known exactly what it was that Jesus had said and done during His time on earth. He said the New Testament I had given him those three decades earlier was the blessing and encouragement he needed to get out of his depression and move on with his life.

One of our most outstanding converts was Pastor Martinez. I met him at a local carpentry shop, became his customer and friend and persuaded him to accept Christ. Ultimately he became one of our finest pastors.

Unfortunately, his wife Mercedes was not always sane. She was not violent, but occasionally she would forget who she was and where she lived and just wander off somewhere. Several times her husband reluctantly put her in an asylum. Finally she disappeared from there and was never found again. Her husband eventually remarried and had a more stable home life.

Pastor Martinez had a tremendous gift for memorization and was a great prayer warrior. He was the one in our group who often suggested we pray for the sick. Many of our people experienced miraculous healings.

During the 1940s, in the bloody political uprisings and purgings, churches were bombed and many of the faithful were killed. Pastor Martinez was among them. He and his elders were holding a prayer meeting in his office at the church one morning when a group of rebels broke in, found them all on their knees in prayer and shot each man in the back of the head.

Why the Lord allowed this martyrdom we do not know, but this kind of violence was not uncommon in Colombia in the middle 1940s.

Excerpted from "Colombia, South America," a report of the Foreign Secretary to the General Council of 1939, *The Alliance Weekly*, July 29, 1939:

The missionaries have carried on steadfastly and zealously. Mr. Taylor, who is in charge of the Bible institute in Armenia, writes: "There seems to be a direct ratio between God's blessing and Satan's interference, and thus we would expect to see a real growth in the work. Even though Satan has attacked the missionaries, the Lord has opened many new doors, and the government continues to guarantee complete liberty of worship in nearly all our districts. This has meant that missionaries and native workers have been able to reach farther into these untouched regions for which we are responsible. At least five large regions within our territory still re-

main neglected. Two of these are so fanatical
that the Lord Himself will have to break
down opposition before much can be accomplished.

"We have succeeded in establishing the full
course of study for the preparation of native
workers and teachers. This standard course
consists of three-and-a-half years of study beyond the preparatory work. Each year has
two three-month sessions of study and an
equal time of vacation for practical work.
During [this time] they have been scattered
until almost every corner [of Colombia] has
been touched at least once by a student."

21

Miracles at the Bible Institute

Although we had perhaps 100 house churches sprinkled throughout the valley, we had only three chapels. But the Lord was blessing our ministry of preparing evangelists by presenting them with Scripture and indepth study in order for them to grow spiritually.

We conducted classes for men and women, boys and girls. Ruth worked with the women, and I and my helpers taught the men. Ruth also oversaw the kitchen operations which grew considerably as people came from too far away to travel home after lessons. So slowly but surely we grew from a day school to a boarding school, and our class terms grew from a matter of days to a matter of weeks.

We soon got word from headquarters in New York that they wanted us to expand our program so that converts from all over Colombia could be taught there. As I look back on it now, I believe that as our Colombian missionary work expanded, gradually we stopped making disciples and started making scholars.

Money to build the Bible Institute came from many sources. We wrote to friends back in the United States and checks poured in, often to the dollar we needed.

We located a plot of land that we thought would be ideal. The price was the equivalent of $4,000, far more money than we had accumulated. So we took our request to the Lord. One day we got a check in the mail from R.G. LeTourneau for exactly $4,000. We felt certain that the Lord intended for us to use it to purchase the property and to apply the money we had received from other donors toward building supplies.

We also received some local donations. One came from the patriarch of a very large family. He had homesteaded his land nearly forty years earlier. In the following decades he purchased more land around his own and, as his family grew, he would turn over plots of his highly prosperous coffee plantation to his sons and daughters when they got married. Now, with all his family living nearby, he invited me to visit him.

When I arrived for the meeting, he had them all assembled, perhaps fifty or more. I told them about our needs and he motioned for me to follow him into his bedroom. There he pulled out a trunk from under the bed and opened it. It was full of gold! The contents of this unpretentious trunk looked like pirate's treasure, although knowing this man to be honest I'm sure he had earned it. He scooped out handfuls of coins and handed them to me, at least fifty or sixty. Sometime later, he invited me back to his house and again we made a visit to his trunk full of gold.

Even with the $4,000 from Mr. LeTourneau in hand we were unable to buy the land directly because it belonged to the Catholic church. So we found a mediary who bought the land in our behalf, took title to it and then signed it over to us.

The land was about the size of a city block. On one side it dropped off into a ravine about forty feet deep. We designed buildings to accommodate all our needs—dormitories for men and women, a residence for staff workers, apartments for married couples, well-equipped classrooms and other facilities for group meetings and worship.

It was a labor-intensive building project, an object lesson in teamwork and cooperation as the body of Christ. It also illustrated the importance of laying a firm foundation, topping it with a sturdy layer of living space and finishing off the project with a well-supported roof that was impervious to problems. This, of course, was the same principle we were teaching our scholars through the Bible lessons.

First, we sank cement pillars and laid on top of them a foundation of sawed wood. We used bamboo for studs and split bamboo for lath. We had to buy all the wood when it was green and dry it ourselves, so as the money came in we would put the lumber on order. This was a lengthy project, not only because of the funding, but because of the seasons. For example, wood had to be cut at the waning of the moon so the white ants wouldn't feast on it and ruin what might become our joists or beams. Fortunately, our native helpers knew all about these things.

Ruth turned out to be a great worker despite some developing medical problems. I of course recognized that again the Lord had prepared me for this task even as a boy working alongside my father on construction crews.

As areas were finished, Ruth and I took up residence and helped to complete the work whenever we were not teaching classes or caring for our growing family which now included Orletta Jean and Clyde Donald.

We were ready to install the red tile roof when Don Pastor informed me that we would have to delay construction for lack of money.

"We don't have enough to pay the workers," he told me sadly. Our shortfall was $1,400. So we talked to the Lord. We prayed that our supporters in the U.S. would sense the need to raise funds and would send money immediately.

A few days went by with no labor. By Thursday not a single check had arrived. And there was no use going to the post office on Friday because we never got foreign mail on Fridays. And yet on that particular Friday something (Someone?) told me to go to the post office anyway.

I found one envelope waiting for me, a foreign letter that had been misrouted around Colombia for at least a week before reaching us. I ripped it open. Sure enough, it contained a check for exactly $1,400. At times like those I often thought the Lord must have a tremendous sense of humor. I could just as easily have had that check a few days earlier but the Lord permitted it to wander around awhile so I would have to trust Him and wait until the last minute.

We finished construction in 1939. Ruth's sister Betty had joined us in the school project. Betty's presence added a great deal to every aspect of the ministry. She invested almost forty years of her life in the Bible Institute.

Ruth and I were not able to return to Colombia as missionaries after 1941. Both of us had developed severe health problems. At one point, Ruth had to be hospitalized to have her appendix removed. She recovered nicely, but while she was there something terrible happened that we didn't learn about until later. Hospitals did not use mosquito nets and she was bitten by an Anopheles species that carries a very rare type of the malaria bacteria. Over the next several years Ruth's heart would race and she suffered frequent dizzy spells, often fainting up to seven times a day. Doctors were confused about what it was because she did not have the fever and chills normally associated with malaria.

I took her back to the doctor who had removed her appendix. He detected such a powerful pulse that he concluded her problems were heart-related. He sent me out of his office with a prescription to fill. While he and Ruth were waiting for me to return, she suddenly had one of these fainting attacks. Witnessing firsthand what we were talking about, he grabbed some test plates and took several smears of blood which he examined under a microscope. When I returned, he smiled at me like a kid with a new toy.

"Clyde," he said, "I've got here the prettiest slides I've ever seen." What he had concluded was that she had such a rare type of malaria that hers was only the second case he had seen in his twenty-five years in Colombia! This was one of the factors that led to our decision to leave the mission field permanently.

Also we both had contracted typhoid. While we had always been very diligent about boiling our drinking water, for years we had been washing our toothbrushes in faucet water without thinking about the inconsistency. We contracted typhoid through a man who fell into the city water reservoir and drowned. He had suffered from a terrible case of typhoid, including high fever and loss of his mind. Left to himself one day, he wandered to the highest point in the city where the reservoir was located. He climbed over the fence, fell into the water and drowned. Naturally, his body contaminated the supply and caused a typhoid epidemic in Armenia.

One of the strangest illnesses I had came as a result of bedbugs. I got chewed up so badly on one overnight trip that I counted 500 bites on one leg. I developed a high fever which did not let up for about ten days and within a matter of three or four days I lost thirty pounds. The one good thing about that particular illness is that if you survive it—and many children do not—then you are immune. Later I was given a bottle which contained the only known remedy—arsenic. Because I was by then over the illness, I kept it handy in case we ever needed it for Ruth. Unfortunately, we did.

After one night away from home she also got a number of bedbug bites and eventually developed the fever. I took her to a doctor. He seemed to know what he was doing and treated

her with arsenic. I assumed he had given her
the right dosage but, in fact, being accustomed
to treating big men who were laborers at the
gold mine in his town, he had given Ruth the
same dosage. It sent her into something like
delirium tremens. Sometimes she would see
and hear beautiful music and then suddenly
she would imagine there were snakes and spi-
ders crawling on the ceiling. The doctor figured
out what he had done wrong and reduced the
dosage. But arsenic is a metal and certain bodies cannot eliminate it. Ruth suffered the after-
effect for many years.

We had peace about leaving Armenia. Ruth
and I had spent nearly ten years of our lives
there seeking out those who were receptive to
God's Word, discipling them and teaching
them how to spread the Word to their coun-
trymen. And the Lord had been gracious to
us by teaching us how to live on a day-by-day,
minute-by-minute basis in His presence, in
His will and for His sake.

Years later, it became clear to me how the
groundwork laid in South America equipped me
for every subsequent challenge of my life.

Tender Tree of Truth

An insecure child in want of strength
  need not search far
For a man of immense love, a giant
  worthy of eternal admiration,
Walked uprightly before her taming a
  steep, rocky path.

He set a precedent of values while
  bearing the load of persecution,
Grounded in Truth and armed with
  prayer, he endured.

Motivated with divine purpose and fitted
  with a pure heart,
He braved the jungle of man's depravity to
Introduce to native man lasting freedom
  and security.

Calloused, work-worn hands gently lifted
  and swung laughing children.
Heavy feet laced in work boots trudged
  many a treacherous mile
While supporting a firm, broad trunk and
  muscled limbs
That seemed to stretch out interminably.

His mere presence demanded respect
  from his peers.
Within his weathered face, chiseled fea-
  tures highlighted eyes bright with zeal,

Eyes smiling on the weak with hope, and
   on the righteous with understanding.

Rock-security, life-sharing tree, great man
   of Providence, silent encourager.
The massive body of this tender giant
   housed a humongous heart.

Undefiled love evidenced itself in every
   action he performed.
Through him this child secured direction,
   hope and faith.

By Danielle Tate, granddaughter
of Clyde and Ruth Taylor

Epilogue

By Orletta Taylor Gillikin

The institute grew and changed much during my years in Armenia, beginning in 1937, working with Clyde and Ruth. The school is now a seminary located in Bogotá and Cali for training ministers.

The property that Clyde and Ruth developed is a thriving congregation of The Christian and Missionary Alliance. There is also a school for Colombian students serving grades kindergarten through twelve, with 1,500 students enrolled. Thanks to the Lord, I was able to return in 1997 to visit the school, my seventh visit since leaving Colombia.

Betty Marstaller (age 91)
Durham, Maine
Founder of Jorge Isaacs School

Getting Mom well was the main concern on my parents' return to the United States. While she was regaining her health, Dad worked on a

191

master's degree in Spanish literature with a mi-
nor in education so he would be better prepared to lead the institute.

The doctors would not allow Mom to return
to the field, but the Lord opened up a new
ministry for Dad as the pastor of Central Baptist Church (Baptist General Church Conference) in Quincy, Massachusetts. Here was the
challenge of a great youth and radio ministry.
As a result of his work, many young people
went into full-time ministry as pastors or missionaries. Also, when the church faced control
of its broadcasting by the Federal Council of
Churches, Dad united with other evangelical
broadcasters for fair representation.

In God's plan, Dad was the man He wanted to
operate the Washington, D.C. office of public
affairs for the newly formed National Association of Evangelicals. This was a venture of faith.
Dad often commented that, before he went to
work there, all he knew about government was
what he had learned in ninth grade civics class.

However, many other people lacked an understanding of how our government operates.
Dad held seminars for college students, pastors
and lay leaders to introduce them to the work-
ings of the federal government and its agencies. Because he piqued their interest, many
evangelicals went into government employ-
ment or became active in local and national
politics. From our own family, brother Clyde
went into the foreign service.

In 1944 we moved to the Washington, D.C. area. In the spring, our sister Darlene was born, followed two years later by Carolyn. In the years that followed, Darlene and Carolyn provided much needed company for Mom while Dad traveled. We also like to say the younger girls kept our parents young!

In addition to becoming accustomed to what he called the "alphabet soup of agency names," Dad built up a network of Christians and other sympathetic personnel in the various agencies where he had to turn for help with passports, export permits and military deferments. One evening, while he was speaking in a Washington church, he mentioned that a key official in a certain agency was retiring and that he wouldn't have a contact there after the man left. At the end of the service a parishioner came up, handed Dad his business card and said, "I'm your man!"

Missions was clearly Dad's first love. While covering many miles and traveling to more than 100 countries, he used every transportation contrivance imaginable to visit missionaries. Besides the encouragement he brought to them, he was able to get a feel for their opportunities for ministry and what they needed to enable them to reach the lost more effectively.

Throughout his travels, many students at colleges, retreats and conferences answered God's call as Dad challenged them to serve Christ wherever He would lead them.

His travels were enjoyable, but also a challenge. After spending many hours on trains and airplanes, Dad knew which seat to reserve so his long legs wouldn't cramp. Mom became his taxi service, often meeting flights in the early morning hours. No matter when we picked him up, having Dad home again was always a treat!

I've found it interesting that each of the four siblings thinks that he or she was Dad's favorite. Dad made each one feel special whether he was spending time teaching us a new skill or just conversing.

Mother was his prime concern due to her poor health. Over the years his "TLC" paid off as her health greatly improved; in 1997, she celebrated her ninety-second birthday.

Their marriage was a joy to observe. She always got the first berry from the garden and he would make a ceremony of presenting her with the year's first rose. Their prayer life was exemplary. As God led them in making decisions, it was done with the certainty that God answers all prayers.

Dad's favorite form of relaxation was gardening. Each home had a vegetable garden plus several species of fruit and berry trees. When they retired, they purchased a home with a half acre of garden space. One of his last requests before he died was to remind the family to spray the fruit trees.

Even in his retirement years, beginning in

1974, he remained active in World Relief and World Evangelical Fellowship. He also spoke at missionary conferences and preached when pastors were away from their pulpits. We were thankful we could spend more time with him and yet grateful that he had much to occupy his attention.

As the cancer took its toll and his hours became numbered, he sat on the edge of the hospital bed with me and my husband on either side of him.

"This is it," he said. "I just can't get up anymore. Let's pray." And with a strong voice he offered to the Lord a beautiful hymn of praise and then he ended his prayer with a plea for the lost of the world to hear the good news.

The next day he met his Lord face-to-face.